SAINT PATRICK

APOSTLE OF IRELAND

SAINT PATRICK
APOSTLE OF IRELAND

HUGH DE BLÁCAM

With a Preface by JOSEPH HUSSLEIN, S.J.

CLUNY
Providence, Rhode Island

CONTENTS

PREFACE (i)

I. *The Boyhood of Patrick* (3)

II. *The Preparation* (19)

III. *"The Voice of the Irish"* (29)

IV. *The Winter at Saul* (44)

V. *The Fires of Slane* (51)

VI. *The Cross Enters Tara* (62)

VII. *The Fall of an Idol* (76)

VIII. *The Faith Wins Connacht* (85)

IX. *Those Who Helped* (100)

X. *Labour and Triumph* (115)

XI. *The Traditional Portrait* (131)

XII. *The Saint and the Tyrant* (142)

XIII. *Retirement* (148)

XIV. *Confession Before Death* (157)

XV. *Ecce Sacerdos Magnus* (176)

EPILOGUE (188)

PREFACE

"Yet, though I am imperfect," wrote St. Patrick at the close of his days, "I wish my brethren and kinsfolk to know the kind of me."[1]

To know the kind of him! That is what every reader wishes to know more fully regarding the great Saint and Apostle of Ireland, mystic and man of action, who came to bring the faith to an entire people, a faith which they have kept inviolate for fifteen centuries.

And yet it is not the man himself so much as the story of his life that perplexes the historian. A dozen pages in Latin sum up the documents we possess from him in his own hand. The earliest biography of him, if we may so call it, was not written until two hundred years after his death. Later lives that have come down to us are largely fabulous. Beyond that, what has the historian to rely upon? Some stray records, traditions, legends, from which to gather what facts he can to fit into his mosaic, with the chronology still at times uncertain and the events in part conjectural.

Nonetheless, when all has been said, a marvellously consistent and reliable picture can be given of St. Patrick, as the author's book bears witness. A vivid, realistic, and genuinely historical

---

1.   St. Patrick's *Confession*, see below, Chapter XIV, p. 150.

narrative has been built up by him. Its comparative brevity, in fact, is accounted for by its studied exclusion of the fabulous.

"You have produced, and that with ample evidence," remarked an eminent Irish historical authority, after critically reviewing the manuscript, "*a fuller and more real St. Patrick than has been given in any other book.*" To have merited this honest verdict, from a foremost scholar in the field, must be reckoned as worth all the time and labour lavishly bestowed on this work.

Three things the author sought to convey to his readers: a trustworthy visualisation of the times; a firm grasp of the historically certain work of the saint, as known to modern research; and, lastly, an understanding of the saint's way of thinking and of the nature of his spirituality. The latter characteristics have been illustrated, wherever possible, by St. Patrick's own sayings or by glimpses caught of him in the traditional portrait preserved in the racial mind.

But Ireland, at the earth's end, is not isolated by the author from the rest of civilisation. Contemporary with St. Patrick, as we are made to feel and realize, were St. Augustine in Africa, St. Jerome at Bethlehem, St. Chrysostom in Constantinople, and St. Cyril in Alexandria. What an age of great men!

A widely travelled man was St. Patrick himself, and in particular was he Rome-minded. "Church of the Irish, nay of the Romans!" are his deathless words. "As you are Christians so be ye Romans." The rock to which he would have them cling was the Rock on which alone Christ had built His Church, Peter, holder of the keys.

An age of magnificently great men, it was yet an age of chaotic and abysmal events such as it seemed had not been from the beginning of time. Christian civilisation in Africa was wiped out by the Vandals, never to be revived again. Rome fell, and all the world cried out.

Because of the withdrawal of Roman arms, Britain was laid waste by the then pagan Irish and the boy Patrick dragged off to captivity. Through him Ireland was singled out in the mercy of God to lead in the reconquest of the world for Christ. Does it not look like a divine compensation at the very moment when all seemed lost and Christianity was seemingly doomed to perish? Patrick was not merely the Apostle of Ireland, he was the Man of Providence. Imperfect and ignorant as he accounted himself, he was thereby most fittingly made the tool of a divine design, more vast than we can trace.

It is with redoubled interest, then, that we view the half-clad slave boy, captured in the Irish raid, herding the swine of his pagan master on the hills of Slemish; that we follow his flight, led as he is by mysterious voices, and trace his travels and adventures, until, invested with the episcopal dignity, he returns as God's anointed to the shores of the Gael. Hardly has he safely landed when, like part of a divine Romance, a little pagan boy finds him fast asleep on the Irish coast and gathers the wild flowers of his native land to place in Patrick's bosom. How beautifully symbolical! And it is that very boy on whom in later years falls the mantle of the Prophet. He is made successor to St. Patrick, for on him, too, is bestowed the gift to see with the eyes of the spirit.

Uninvited, Patrick enters the banquet hall of the High-King of Tara, while the harpers cease to strike their chords with songs of olden gods, and the white-clad Druids look at him with fear and stark amazement. A new order has begun, they realize, but the struggle unto death must first be waged. There is no doubt as to the final victor.

So from village to village, from court to court, we follow the true Patrick of history as fifteen hundred years ago his feet pressed the green sod of Ireland, every leaf of which he loved. But more than all he loved the souls of Ireland's sons and daughters, "begotten by me unto Christ, more than I can number." Sweet words, spoken when his body was feeble from labour but his heart was tender as always with love. How like the words of St. Paul: "For if you have ten thousand instructors in Christ, yet not many fathers. For in Christ Jesus, by the gospel, I have begotten you!" (1 Cor. 4:15).

Indeed, between Paul and Patrick there is a strong kinship of souls, alike in their mystical life and their apostolic labours. Both possessed the same strong, fiery nature, ready to do all, dare all, and endure all for Christ. Yes, we know St. Patrick, the true, the real, the historic St. Patrick; and we know him only less definitely and minutely than we know St. Paul, who has given us so much of his own life in his precious epistles.

Finally, to produce a biography of Ireland's great Apostle that should be reliable did not necessitate the elimination of all legendary lore. What it rather implied was a realistic treatment of it. Fiction and fable even, when honestly recognized as such, yield valuable testimony to popular sentiment and not seldom emphasize genuinely historic characteristics. They are popular thought crystallised in poetry. The true historic vision consists in seeing through the golden haze of mist the fiery disk of truth. In all these regards Mr. De Blacam has accomplished a difficult task with charm, discretion, and distinction.

Joseph Husslein, s.j., ph.d.
St. Louis University
December 18, 1940

SAINT PATRICK

APOSTLE OF IRELAND

CHAPTER I

The Boyhood of Patrick

(1) His Native Land

Saint Patrick tells us himself that he was born in Britain; he names a place called Bannavem Taberniae. Nobody knows for sure where this place was. Formerly, it was held by most writers that it was near Dumbarton, in Scotland, then the most northerly Roman strong-hold in Britain, but the chief scholars now favour the Severn valley as the likeliest region. That land of wheat-fields and cider presses, with the tinted curves of the Welsh mountains as background, was a battlefield between Irish raiders and Roman garrison; and here, Dr. Eoin MacNeill holds[1] Patrick was reared. Abergavenny is suggested as the actual site of the saint's home in boyhood.

A few scholars have held that the peninsula of Pembroke was the place of Patrick's birth; and their view has been championed vigorously by Dr. Oliver St. John Gogarty in a book[2] which appeared when the present writer was at work on the present essay. Pembroke, the olden Celtic kingdom of Dyfed, a lovely mountainous headland of granite that is clothed in autumn in a purple

---

1. Eoin MacNeill, "The Birthplace of St. Patrick," *Proceedings of the Royal Irish Academy.*
2. O. St. John Gogarty, *I Follow Saint Patrick.*

vestment of heather—this region has an abiding place in Irish history. It was invaded from Ireland and colonised, in the age when Roman power contracted. There, too, at St. David's, the Welsh saint dwelt from whom the great Irish monastic leaders received inspiration. Later, again, the Anglo-Norman hosts, under the Earl of Pembroke, Strongbow, poured from this end of Britain to invade Ireland and to open the seven hundred years' Iliad of her woes. Geography ordained that Pembroke should be, of old, the place of contact, for better or worse, between Ireland and Britain; for the peaks of Wicklow, a line on the horizon, in which the sun goes down, may be discerned from the hill above St. David's. Up there, a rocky seat is called St. Patrick's chair, and tradition says that he first saw Ireland from that point of vantage. St. Patrick's well and St. Patrick's chapel thereby, formerly were pointed to as the traditional place of the holy youth's baptism. Certainly, tradition and probability are in harmony here.

At any rate, Patrick was born somewhere in Britain, in or about the year 385, in the age when the Roman Empire, the world-state, was decaying, and the extremities were failing. That Empire reached from the Great Wall in Northern Britain, and Dyfed in West Britain, away across the world to Egypt and the Holy Land. Radiating from Rome, roads ran to all the ends of that vast territory, and where the English Channel interrupted the road to the Wall, it was continued in a direct line beyond the short sea-crossing. Those roads were the best ever made until the twentieth century, when, after a long age, the Roman mode of road-making, the packing of small stones and grit between curbs, was revived, to provide highways fit for motor traffic. Posts ran regularly on the Roman roads. Communication was unbroken from Asia Minor to the corners of Spain, and from Sicily to the lowlands of Scotland.

No frontiers divided this prodigious State; no tariff walls checked the natural flow of trade. All educated persons spoke Latin, and Latin was the vernacular of the cities. In fine, the world ruled by the Romans was one country as much as the United States today; and with this difference from the United States, that there existed no other great Power beyond its frontier, no rival. Outside the Roman world there were only barbarian peoples (as the Romans called them), chiefly the Germans and the Irish, neither of whom as yet possessed a material development to compare with Rome's rich artificiality.

The barbarians had no great cities, but the Roman realm had many, besides the mighty capital. In Britain, a Celtic seaport had grown, under the Romans, into *Londinium*, a huge city, much bigger and richer than the London which Shakespeare knew thirteen centuries later. The Roman cities had theatres as splendid as those of today and purveying much the same heathenish amusements, of which the old poets wrote as moralists write of the modern theatre. There were amphitheatres, too, where men fought to the death with sword against net and trident; tigers and elephants were used in bloodthirsty spectacles. The rich lived in palaces, the mosaics of which are dug up sometimes, and had central heating to combat the island climate. Statues of marbles and bronze, sumptuous baths, temples, are unearthed to give us a glimpse of the grandeur that was Rome, even in the British province. The poor-folk dwelt in tenements—huge blocks like those which we build for the poor now—and received doles of free food and free amusement.

The mines of Britain were worked for coal and metals. There was a big export of salt, and many industrial products were imported; all Britain used crockery made in the factories of Gaul. Britain was one of the Empire's main granaries. Shiploads of wheat that was grown in St. Patrick's country, from Pembroke to Kent, were sent to the Continent, to provision the Roman garrisons on the Rhine.

How was the farming done? Rich men lived in country seats called villas. A rural palace of stone, with stables, barns, and huts, formed a villa; the huts housed beasts and fodder, and also men. The men were slaves. Mark that: the toiling throng was made up of human beings, who could be bought and sold. In his writings, St. Patrick talks of the price of men as we talk of the price of cattle.

All that enormous Empire, with its grand cities, its palaces, with panels of ivory and gold, its marbles, aqueducts, thronged roads, basilicas with magistrates dealing out cold-blooded justice, its barracks and camps, its factories, baths, and arenas—all, all, rested on slavery.

A few lived (as a Roman poet said), the rest toiled for them.

Such was the gorgeous, cruel civilisation in which Patrick was born and reared. He lived in Britain until his sixteenth year, a care-free youth, indifferent to sacred things—so he tells us himself. Then came the event that changed his life and changed history.

(2) THE CAPTIVE

It was about the year 400, when the warrior-king, Niall of the Nine Hostages, was monarch of that island to the West, the land that neither the Roman civilisation nor the Christian faith had won; that *terra incognita* whose purple peaks seen from the western shore of Britain were signs of strangeness and wildness, fabulous to the city mind. In that year, several score of Irish ships came from some place of secret mobilisation—Carlingford Lough, very likely—out of the blue distance, where Ireland lay. They were vessels with leather sides and leather sails, sails that were aided by oars which several gigantic men toiled upon. They reached the shallow waters of the Dee to the north, perhaps, or sailed up the Severn Estuary; they beached, and then there leapt ashore the young warriors of Niall. Into the rich West Country, the war-bands swarmed.

Near Shrewsbury is the place where the Roman town of Uricon once stood—a garrison town, built to control the Welsh hillsmen. Into Uricon, the Irish warriors poured, with their long swords that flashed over the few short Roman-British weapons raised against them. Uricon fell, and was given to the flames, and Niall marched on through the glowing ashes, to lead his men to the plunder of the Roman realm.

Somewhere in the area of the Irish raid, be it in the Severn Valley or the Pembroke Peninsula, a comfortable middle-class family dwelt, a family that had come over from Gaul, some say. The head of the house, Calpurnius by name, had a post in a town or suburb, and was well enough off to keep a small out-farm. To the farm, for health or holidays or safety, Calpurnius had sent a sturdy boy of fifteen, his son, in the days when the Irish raiders were going through defenceless Britain. His holiday refuge did not save the lad. Some marauding band came the way of Calpurnius' farm, and the son of Calpurnius heard a strange tongue, the Gaelic, in the shouted orders and boasts and cries of discovery. Some defence was made; for Patrick says the raiders slew servants on the farm who opposed them. The fifteen-year-old lad, however, was seized. He was a likely looking slave. The barbarian Irish had learnt from the example of Roman civilisation that men could be enslaved, bought, sold, made to work for masters like brute beasts.

Through the scorched and frightened land the warbands made

for their ships again. The gigantic Niall watched his gillies carrying sacks of Roman plunder and whipping along young British folk who would bring a price in the slave-trade. There were several thousand prisoners.

It had been an easy raid. The Britons were a race weakened with prosperity and comfort. Roman troops had guarded the land in the barrack towns, but now they had been drawn away, with their shining shields that could be linked in walls of steel, their spears, javelins, swords, and artillery. Aye, it was but a couple of years before this Irish raid that the Twentieth Legion, which for three hundred fifty years had been stationed at Chester to guard the roads to the Dee—that this Legion, which seemed rooted in the land—had been marched away. Rome, we have said, needed her great fighting machine to guard her own land and the home provinces, against the swarming Goths and other barbaric tribes. So she was leaving Britain, the island province, to defend itself— and it lay as an easy prey to the Irish hosts.

The captives—marched to the ships by their Irish captors, while the hearts throbbed with terror in their bosoms, their wounds festered and their wrists chafed under the bonds—saw the broken walls of Roman posts, the ashes of British towns. The fleet at last was laden, the leather sails were hoisted, and the captives knew that they had left the Roman world, perhaps forever. Strong fellows were put to the oars, and laboured under the leather lash, to drag themselves and their friends out over the sea to the strange land of exile, to misty Hibernia, land of forests, wolves, and giant barbarians.

Where the fleet landed, we cannot guess. Niall may have had the secure waters of Carlingford Lough as his naval headquarters. Some strong place like that must have been his base when he prepared the expedition, with ships and men enough for so great an assault on the Roman land. Rich with plunder, the war-bands quickly dispersed. Only twice in ten years could Niall get such a host together.

The son of Calpurnius, carried off by his captors, or else sold to some dealer in flesh and blood, was brought at last to the land that we call Antrim. There he was made a servant to a lord named Meliuc who owned woodland and pasture on the slopes of Slemish, above the great forest which reached across to gleaming Lough Neagh.

They asked the lad his name. "I am Patricius," he answered. They could not get their tongues round the Roman word. They made it Cothrige—that is how Patrick is called in the oldest Life.

Cothrige was sent to mind the herds on the mountain.

(3) ON SLEMISH

For six long years, poor young Cothrige was a slave. He may have changed hands, indeed, in the market, but Meliuc of Slemish is the only master of whom we read. Those were the longest years of life—the teens. The lad must have suffered at first more than happy people can imagine.

Consider: he did not know how his father and mother had fared, or if his brothers and sisters were living after the raid that had torn him away to exile and servitude. Moreover, he had enjoyed a highly civilised rearing, but now he must tend beasts, droves of swine on the bare mountain, at the command of a barbarian of strange tongue. At home he had talked the Latin of the British towns, and had been familiar with the P-Celtic vernacular of the Britons, now represented by Welsh. In Ireland, he heard no Latin, but only that Q-Celtic speech, the Gaelic, in which the British P's and B's became K and Q, and his proud Roman-British name, as we have seen, was corrupted into Cothrige. The difference between the Celtic language of the Britons and that of the Gaels was not so great then as the present difference between Welsh and Irish (which are about as far different as English from German)—it was, perhaps, about the same as between Italian and Portuguese. The two belonged to the same linguistic family, but were far from mutually intelligible. During his years in Antrim, Cothrige became, of necessity, an Irish speaker. That was providential, but what suffering was entailed by this apprenticeship to Irish nationality!

Barbarians, these Irish masters were. It was so that the highly civilised British-Roman had been trained to regard them. Here were no stone mansions with gilded panelling and Greek vases. Here was no *villa* but a *baile*; that is, a collection of dab-and-wattle huts, plastered and limewashed, within a circular earthen rampart. He had been reared in the house of a well-to-do British citizen; that means, in a house which was heated in winter by steam that ran through hollow tiles. Now he was sheltered from the clouds that blew on a northern mountain by nothing better than some shieling under the rocks, such as sheep use. He saw no cities, churches, shops, theatres, post-horses, books, but trampled court-yards through which companies of hunters moved, with leashes of mighty wolfhounds.

Yet that rugged Irish life had a fascination that virile folk always have preferred to the glamour of cities. There was no hunger there. Food was not doled out for purchase; it was as plentiful as Nature's gifts—fresh milk, cheeses, strength-giving grain, venison, salmon from the teeming rivers. Sport was plentiful, and laughter, and the loveliness of the smokeless land. Down the ages, that order of things—the big house of the lord, with his craftsmen and land-workers and huntsmen grouped around him in a *baile* that a white retaining wall made into a little self-subsistent community—was refined by Christianity, enriched by the arts and by learning; it kept its character as long as Gaels were Gaels. Twelve, thirteen, and fourteen hundred years after Patrick's day, poets who were masters of Greek called the Gaels "the Greeks of the West,"[3] and lamented bitterly the destruction of a life most dear to the race. Egan O Rahilly, for example, in an elegy for the O Callaghan of the early eighteenth century[4] describes a Gaelic household in Munster—the "musical, kingly house," with its doors opening upon courts of amber light, its airy chambers and laden tables, its chess-playing warriors, feasters, scholars, and clergy and great folk conversing on the princes of Europe; he tells how the horn would sound on the plain and the heavy cry of the chase descend from the sides of misty hills, how foxes and red bucks, hares, water-hens and pheasants would be started, and how the lord's hounds and men would return wearied from the uplands; and how now the voice of appreciative foreigners was loud in the happy dwelling, *glór na n Gall go teann śan ór-bhrugh*, as the old order passed away. Only in the Scottish Highlands, where the chiefs bought survival by selling their faith, the old life lingered into the nineteenth century, and was depicted by engravers of scenes of Highland bothies and gillies bringing home the deer.

For company, young Cothrige had his master's children, as tradition tells. No doubt, they ran out on fine days to play under the

---

3.   Owen Roe O'Sullivan, *Amhrain Eoghain Ruaidh Ui Shuilleabhain.*
4.   *Poems of Aodhagan O Rathaille*, edited Rev. P. Dinneen.

serving lad's eyes; perhaps they were part of his care. We can guess
how he got scanty news of the world from their childish prattle
about their elders' talk. They would tell him, one day, how great
Niall of the Hostages, the raiding king whose warriors had made
Cothrige captive years before, had gone on an expedition to Gaul,
to plunder that province as Britain had been plundered:

"But he was killed, Cothrige!"

"The Gauls slew him?"

"No, but an Irish traitor took the King's life."

It was somehow thus that Cothrige must have learnt of the
growing ruin of the Roman realm. Gaul was attacked now, and not
by Irish raiders alone, but by swarms of Goths and Vandals, warriors from the Germanic lands afar. Across the south of Gaul, and
into Spain, that country of vineyards, the race whose very name
sounded uncouth, was advancing, looting towns, seizing lands,
settling in the best lands. Rome was recalling her last legions from
Britain to hold Gaul—then to hold Italy—nay, but the city itself.

The Roman world is ending!

So the Irish children would tell Cothrige, with little vaunting
voices, repeating what they had heard the chiefs at their father's
table say. The barbarian peoples had good cause to hate the pagan
empire which now was coming to its end.

That empire's history was one of peace that was no peace—
peace built on subjection of nations, the enslavement of man. It
had begun when Julius Caesar, before Christ was born, hacked his
way to greatness through the bodies of the Gaulish Celts. A million men perished, a million were sold into slavery, so Plutarch
affirms, when Caesar crushed the Gallic peoples. Vercingetorix,
the first Celtic patriot, whose line comes down to Pearse and Ter-
ence McSwiney, offered his life for his nation's peace; and Caesar

sent this noble chief, *anima naturaliter Christiana*, away to Rome to be dragged in shame through the mocking streets in a Triumph, imprisoned for years, and then done to death. Nor was Caesar content to be thus merciless to his betters, but he wrote his war despatches, his *de Bello Gallico*, to slander the people he subdued, alleging that they practised human sacrifice and representing them as savages; war propaganda of the kind always practised by conquerors of Caesar's kind. There is no other evidence of human sacrifices of the decent Gauls; but it is historic fact that Caesar's people sacrificed their captives to their own ugly Roman gods.

After Gaul, Britain had been subdued. If Gaul had a Vercingetorix to fight and suffer pre-Christian martyrdom for justice's sake, Britain had its warrior-queen, Boadicea, to be scourged by Roman rods for loving liberty. A century after Caesar, Agricola mastered the northerly parts of Britain, "and lined the coast, which lies opposite to Ireland, with a body of troops; not so much from an apprehension of danger," Tacitus tells us,[5] "as with a view to future projects." In the year 82 a petty Irish king, flying from some dispute, "was received by the Roman general, and, under a show of friendship, detained to be of use on some future occasions. I have often heard Agricola declare," his son-in-law continues, "that a single legion, with a moderate band of auxiliaries, would be sufficient to complete the conquest of Ireland. Such an event, he said, would contribute greatly to bridle the stubborn spirit of the Britons, who, in that case, would see with dismay the Roman arms triumphant, and every spark of liberty extinguished round their coast."

A revolt behind his lines caused Agricola to give up his plan for the invasion of Ireland, but the threat remained, and was known

---

5. Tacitus, *Agricola*.

to the rulers of Ireland. In the third century, when Roman power was at its height, the first great Irish High-King, Cormac mac Airt—he was a Christian by desire—made military roads, organised the Fianna Eireann as a national army, encamped at Tara, and other kings of his century copied the Roman system of earthen frontier walls. Ireland was prepared for defence, but the Roman attack never came, and the Fenian bands that were to have resisted invasion were turned, in the fourth century, to the opposite use. It was the Roman threat of centuries that provoked the attacks which culminated in Niall's campaigns of depredation.

Such were the relations of the Roman world with Ireland and other barbarian lands, between which there existed, it seems, a common enmity to the empire.[6] We are safe in assuming, therefore, that the Irish folk who told Cothrige of the Roman defeats vaunted as they spoke; but pangs surely went through the slave-boy's heart.

The world that had bred him was ending! At home in Britain, among the Imperial folk who were Christians in name, but little more, he had given no thought to grave things. Now, on the hills of exile, his bent of mind was changed: so he has written for us to read. He never could hear Mass now. He was shut from the sacraments, broken in soul; but he turned to the inner life as an exile turns to home. His life became mystical. The ragged swineherd grew into one of the great contemplatives of history.

He tells how he lived in prayer, day and night. He chose to sleep, not within the rampart of the *dun*, but out under trees, or on the rocky mountainside, in frost, rain, and storm. This he did in order that he might perfect his spiritual life. When dawn broke

---

6.   Eoin MacNeill, *Early Irish Laws and Institutions*, Chapter 1.

through cold, grey Irish skies on Slemish, Cothrige had already risen from sleep to begin the day in a rapture of contemplation.

This we read in his own words, written fifty years later. He describes those fasts and watchings in exile which lasted six years, and tells how at last (like St. Joan later) he heard a strange Voice.

"Well are you fasting," the Voice said, "soon now you will go to your father-land."

This message in sleep told Cothrige that he was to return to his *patria*; that is, to the Roman, the Christian world. After a short while, the Voice spoke again, and said: "Behold, your ship is ready."

So, one day the slave-boy was not found when the farm folk sought him. The swine were astray, their watcher gone, none knew where. Somewhere down the Tara road a stripling of twenty years, brown and hard as a wild creature, was striding along, making southward to where, two hundred miles distant, he knew from his vision that a ship would be found, bound for the Roman land.

(4) The Flight

All roads led to Rome, in the Roman world. In the Irish world, all roads led to Tara, and very good roads they were. Along the highway from the north to Tara, probably in the year 407 or 408, the stripling Cothrige went; for we must assume that he followed the trunk roads of the country. The forests that cling to Slieve Gullion's side were full of strange light as he left the grand mountain to his right hand, and within another hour he would pass under Faughart Hill, with its fort on the summit, the sentry over the road into the Leinster plain.

Had he prophetic knowledge of a girl, a slave like himself, who soon would be reared in that fort, Brigid her name?

The road crossed the Leinster plain and took Cothrige past the hill that would be called Ardpatrick in after days. Perhaps there were great scholars at some bardic school in that place, who saw a slave-boy going by, and little guessed that he would give his name to the place, when they were forgotten. After another long day's march, Cothrige would go down a wooded glen to where the Boyne spread its broad waters, and the kingfisher flashed beside the stakes of the ford. That was the scene where a huge battle had been waged, four hundred years earlier, when the hosts of the north came down to Rosnaree on the Boyne. Perhaps, Cothrige watched the riverside battlefield with interest, as we watch it now, recalling another, a later Battle, that of the Boyne.

Next Cothrige made for Duleek, across the river, and now the blue and green expanses of Meath were around him, and he delighted in the Royal land, so rich in crops (in those days), so kingly in its beauty.

Traffic was greater here. Often great chariots rolled past him, and he took to the roadside grass. Mystic though he was, and withdrawn in thought, he must have asked himself what princes, what scholars, poets, rich men, were these who passed him on the highway to Tara—Tara, with its earthen ramparts and buildings with high timber walls, lime bright; its manners, its crowded smaller dwellings on the lower slopes, thatched huts like bee-skeps, a scene of life and liveliness that now he saw for the first, but not the last, time in his strange career! Tara was a considerable town then. Beside the king's people, the hospitallers, artificers, lawyers, and the like, there were all manner of strange folk and trades. Maybe Cothrige rested there. It would be easy. Many a foreign captive, now grown to a petty tradesman, would have a corner in his hut for the runaway, a Briton and a Christian and a slave.

Out from Tara by one of the roads to the South, Cothrige pressed on his way. Perhaps he took the road of the Hurdle Ford, that went through our Dublin and led on over the blue curves of the hills into the exhausted goldfields of Wicklow. If he went that way, Arklow might be his destination. Some scholars think that Cothrige reached Wexford, going by this route. Others believe that he did not touch Dublin or Wicklow, but took the other great southern road from Tara, which went from Tara due south to Naas, thence by the valley of the Barrow to *Dinn Righ*, the capital of South Leinster, which we call Leighlinbridge—and so to the navigable waters. Whether at Arklow, or Wexford, or Waterford, the ship of his dream was there before him, a vessel just about to sail for the Roman world.

It was an Irish vessel, probably. It bore in its cargo great Irish wolfhounds. These dogs were the chief export of Ireland to the Roman world. A letter exists, written a few years before Cothrige's adventure, in which a Roman noble describes these *Scottici canes*, which were so mighty that it was thought that they must be carried in iron cages.

Moorings had been cast, when the lean, brown, runaway slave appeared and cried to the captain that he must be taken abroad. He was refused. This was a blow to his confidence in his Voice. He turned away and walked along the quay, and he prayed as he walked.

Before his prayer was finished, a cry came to him from the ship: "Come, we'll take you and trust you." The ship's masters had changed their minds. We do not know why, but it may be that they had bethought themselves that this slave-boy, who could talk Latin, would be useful as interpreter in the Roman land; he was accustomed to animals, too, and would be helpful with the hounds.

So Cothrige went abroad, and the ship floated out from Irish waters, with the exile freed at last. Three days that ship was on the seas, with its rugged heathen seamen and their great caged wolfhounds and Cothrige the swineherd; its leather sail drawing, its oars beating the grey waves, and then, like a new world found, the coasts of Gaul appeared—and the seafarers came ashore in a land made white by recent war, a land of desolation, hunger, and fear.

Cothrige had come home to a land where he would be Patricius once again, if people lived; but it seemed that all were dead.

CHAPTER II

The Preparation

(1) In Gaul

All the land was white with ruin; war had passed that way. The little company of seafarers from Ireland set out, with their gigantic, shaggy wolfdogs, hoping to find a market for them in one of the Roman cities of the South. Doubtless, the market had been good since Quintus Aurelius Symmachus, a Roman ex-consul, about a dozen years earlier, had written to his brother Flavianus:

> *Editioni muneris nostri et usitata a te et insolita conferuntur....* You provide both what is usual and unusual for helping our display, being both a generous provider for our annual ceremonies and a discoverer of new things; and this is proved by your offering of seven Irish dogs, at which Rome was so astonished on the day of the rehearsal that they thought they must have been brought in iron cages.[1]

The hopes of the travellers sank, however; for the war-swept land was a wilderness. They were a month on the road without

---

1. Symmachus, *Epistola* II.

finding supplies of food—so Patrick relates—and actually were obliged to leave some of their dogs dying of hunger on the way.

The captain began to abuse the only Christian of the company.

"What sayst thou, Christian?"—it is so that Patrick gives his words.—"Thy God is great and almighty; why then can you not pray for us?—for we are in danger of starvation. It will be hard for us if ever we see a human being again."

Patricius spoke plainly to those pagans. "Turn earnestly and with all your hearts to the Lord my God, to whom nothing is impossible," he said, "that He may send you food for your journey until you be filled; for everywhere he hath abundance."

So the swineherd prayed, and those pagans added their pleas to his, no doubt; and behold!—a drove of swine came through the desert. The surviving wolfdogs, we may guess, were used to capture them; the knives worked, and the company got food enough. Two days the men and dogs rested at that place. "Thereafter," Patrick says of his companions, "they gave greatest thanks to God, and I became honoured in their eyes." They now found food in plenty. Wild honey they came upon, but one of them offered this to heathen gods, and Patricius refused to partake of it.

One night in the war-made desert, Patricius suffered temptation of the mind. Nearly fifty years later, when, as an aged and retired bishop, he wrote an account of these adventures, the horror still was overpowering. "Satan tempted me strongly, which I shall remember as long as I am in this body." What was this temptation? Perhaps we can find the answer in something told by a present-day missionary, also Patrick by name, concerning an experience in Africa. He was alone, one night, and remembered that all folk of the land for miles around were heathen; their minds were remote from his, and he was a stranger among them. The loneliness, he afterwards said, was more horrible than any nightmare; the utter absence of spiritual sympathy must be known to be believed; it shakes the soul. Is not the first Patrick's suffering made clear by the words of his late successor? The desolation of the Roman land brought the homelessness down on poor young Patrick. For six years he had lived among such pagans as his present companions, but he had rested his mind on the memory of Christian lands. Now, in Gaul, where the Goths and Vandals had blotted out life, it seemed that the Christian world itself had perished; and here was he, the last Christian, a castaway.

His sorrows were not ended. A war-band, perhaps of Vandals, came upon the Irish company and took them all prisoners. "So, after many years of slavery, I was a slave yet again," Patrick writes. However, after two months, "the Lord delivered me out of their hands," he says. Somehow, Patricius won to freedom, in the south of the land that we now call France.

(2) THE EXAMPLE OF ST. AMBROSE

He travelled France and Italy, begging or working his way. He was using his opportunity to educate himself for the mysterious destiny which he believed himself to possess, although he did not know yet for what special purpose he had been carried through such strange adventures, of body and of soul. He may have walked to Rome! he may have gone through that city as a wandering boy, where later he was to be received as a great bishop.

It is almost certain that he went to Milan, which lately had been the Imperial capital, and there he heard tell of the mighty Bishop Ambrose, who had died a few years earlier. He must have been intensely interested in what St. Ambrose achieved. Indeed, the acts of Ambrose foreshadowed his own.

The former Bishop of Milan, who died away back in 374, had been an Arian—he had given countenance to that heresy sweeping through the Roman world with the Barbarian hosts, which denied the doctrine of the Trinity. The Imperial City was convulsed by feuds; for Catholic orthodoxy and Arian heresy were taken up as party causes. Milan was like Belfast in the time of Orange riots. A Governor, Ambrosius by name, not yet baptised, but a Christian catechumen, was sent by the Roman prefect to assert good order, entered the church and spoke to conflicting parties of the benefits of peace and tranquillity in the State. Hardly had he finished speaking, when a boy cried out: "Ambrose! Bishop!"—and the multitude took up the cry, "Ambrose! Bishop!"—a demand which was carried to the Emperor Valentinian himself. Persuaded by *vox populi* and the Emperor's wishes, the just Governor at length assented. He was baptised, and in eight days received Orders culminating in those of the episcopacy. Such was the strange election and rise of St. Ambrose, Bishop, Confessor, and Doctor of the Church. In his exalted office, the governor-made-bishop showed himself the spiritual master even of successive emperors. He frustrated the demand, which an Arian empress-mother favoured, to set up the idol of Victory in the Senate House; a Christian would honour no abstract deities. *Causa religionis est*, he said, and his will overbore the Court. Later, when the Arians asked that one of the city's basilicas be granted to them, and the Bishop was brought before the Court and bidden to admit the Emperor's jurisdiction, Ambrose answered:

"The Emperor is within the Church and not above the Church."

The Arians, he said, "were willing to surrender to Caesar the right to rule the Church"—the worst of heresies.

Ambrose won. By his goodness, he persuaded many Arians; by his strength, he defeated the rest. He compelled Theodosius, after a crime, to public penance. When he died in 397, he left Catholicism secure, even at the head of the secular world. On his faith and will, Arianism in the Empire was broken. The Roman world soon was to sink in ruin, but the Roman Church was to stand, secure, unde- filed; Ambrose was the Holy Spirit's agent to that end.

"St. Ambrose," writes a late historian, "is very literally an epoch-making figure. Thanks to his personality, to the accident that made the very centre of the world's affairs the stage on which his personality was displayed, to his gifts as writer and speaker, his life set the pattern for all the next thousand years of the relations between the Catholic bishop and the Catholic prince."[2]

This lesson Patrick must have taken to heart as he heard the story of Ambrose from churchmen who were full of it.

"In these few years at Milan," the author continues, "he laid the foundations in his careful demarcation of the rights of *religio* and *respublica*, of all the public law of the *respublica Christiana* of the coming Middle Ages. Theodosius, though neither Emperor nor Bishop realised it, was to be the last Emperor to rule effectively the lands between the Atlantic and the Adriatic. Slowly increasing and inevitable chaos was to descend upon that vast heritage. One of the few things to survive was the Catholic episcopate, and it survived as formed in the mould of Ambrose of Milan."

Here was a mighty saint and statesman of the Church, truly!— yet how near to humble Christian souls of all lands and times we perceive from the "Prayer of St. Ambrose" that we find in our prayer books still:

---

2.   Philip Hughes, *A History of the Church*, Volume I.

O loving Lord Jesus Christ, I a sinner, not presuming on mine own merits, but trusting in Thy mercy and goodness, approach with fear and trembling to the table of Thy most sweet feast. I have both heart and body stained with many sins, neither have I kept strict guard over my thoughts and my tongue. Wherefore, O gracious God, O awful majesty, I, a wretched creature entangled in difficulties, have recourse to Thee the fount of mercy; to Thee do I hasten that I may be healed, and take refuge under Thy protection, and I ardently desire to have Him as my Saviour, whom I am unable to withstand as my judge.

The humility is like Patrick's, and the very language, too. "*Ego, Patricius peccator...*"

(3) The End of a World

It was in the year 410, thirteen years after the death of St. Ambrose, and while Patricius was a young man in France or Italy, that an event took place which shook all the world, as a street is shaken when some mighty building falls. Rome itself, the head of the world, fell.

Alaric, the Visigoth, had demanded of Rome the land between the Danube and the Gulf of Venice as a patrimony, and to be made the Imperial Commander-in-Chief. Rome was strengthened by legions from the east, and the Teutonic war-lord, thus defied, swept down upon the City, and burst its northern gates. Barbarian warriors swarmed into the City of cities, and plundered the seat of the world's power, a thing unheard of, that was like the end of the world. That is exactly how it seemed to the two greatest church-men, greatest intellects, of that time—souls to whom St. Patrick was to be the successor and peer.

The first of these was St. Jerome, then dwelling in Bethlehem, whither he had retired from Rome a quarter of a century earlier, to pursue the life of monastic devotion, meditation, and scholarship. Jerome, having recently completed his sublime Vulgate version of the Scriptures, was at work on commentaries on the Prophets. While he wrote on Ezechiel, he heard the tidings of the fall of the City that he had forsaken, and wrote—

"I was so stupefied and dismayed that day and night I could think of nothing but the welfare of the Roman community. It seemed to me that I was sharing the captivity of the saints and I could not open my lips until I received some more definite news. All the while, full of anxiety, I wavered between hope and despair, torturing myself with the misfortune of others. But when I heard that the bright light of all the world was quenched, or rather that the Roman Empire had lost its head and that the whole universe had perished in one city: then, indeed, '*I became dumb and humbled myself and kept silence from good words.*'"

Two years later, Jerome wrote again: "A dreadful rumour came from the West. Rome was besieged, and its citizens forced to buy their lives with gold. Then thus despoiled they were attacked a second time, so as to lose their lives as well as their substance. My voice sticks in my throat, and even as I dictate this letter sobs choke my utterance. The City which had taken the whole world was itself taken; nay, more, famine anticipated the sword, and but few citizens were left to be made prisoners. In their frenzy, the starving people had recourse to hideous food and tore each other limb from limb that they might have flesh to eat."

We can recognise the voice of Jerome when Rome fell as well as that of the Hebrew prophet whom he translated, when we read his majestic Latin:

> *Juxta est dies Domini magnus,*
> *Juxta est et velox nimis:*
> *Vox diei Domini amara,*
> *Tribulabitur ibi fortis.*
> *Dies irae, dies illa,*
> *Dies tribulationis et angustiae,*
> *Dies calamitatis et miseriae,*
> *Dies tenebrarum et caliginis,*
> *Dies nebulae et turbinis:*
> *Dies tubae et clangoris super civitates munitas*
> *Et super angulos Excelsos.*[3]

The second great mind that was shaken by the news of Rome's fall was St. Augustine, convert and disciple of St. Ambrose, and now Bishop of Hippo where he was at once the pillar of the Church in Africa and the theologian whose writings were to teach the whole Church, to the end of time. Saving St. Paul and St. Thomas Aquinas, the Church never had a mightier intellect in its service than this already world-famed churchman in Africa, aged 56 when "the aboriginal dogma, the rock of the old world's creed, Rome Eternal, crumbled. Augustine," we read,[4] "being implored from all

---

3   "The great day of the Lord is near: it is near and exceeding swift…a day of wrath, a day of tribulation and distress, a day of calamity and misery…a day of the trumpet and alarm against the fenced cities and against the high bulwarks."

4   Hughes, *A History of the Church*, Volume I.

parts of the Empire to give some explanation of the break-up of the old world in spite of the coming of Christ, rose in a moment to the vision of the supreme City, the better Rome, the holiest Jerusalem, which is the Catholic Church, over against which is set the earthly city of the devil, the empire of the enemies of God." The heir of all the ancient world's learning was appalled when the visible Rome proved mortal; then rose to the greatest thought of the ages. Rome, dedicated to eternity, had fallen, but the City of God lived. This idea Augustine developed in his master work, his *De Civitate Dei*, one of the world's three or four greatest books. He began writing while Jerome in Bethlehem still was dumb with amazement, and he worked for thirteen years in the elaboration of his vast conception. With Augustine's *City of God*, the Church of antiquity was liberated from temporal fears, and set its eyes, as the Classical world dissolved, on the world yet to be. It has been said well that, "Just as she was about to be gathered in silence to Assyria and Babylon, Europe lived anew, simply and solely by reason of that unquenchable hope, the unsurrendering Christian spirit, so powerfully manifested in St. Augustine's writing."

Thus, three of the grandest minds of all ages flourished when our Patricius still was young, unknown, uncalled to his own high task. Of exactly one mind with these giants, Ambrose, Jerome, Augustine, was the as yet almost nameless young fellow, who turned in those days to an island in the Roman sea—Lérins, where the wind blows through palms in misty sunlight—to visit monks, and to become one of them. A world had crashed down, barbarians were lords of Europe, yet the young monk with the mind of Ambrose, Jerome, Augustine, was he who would build a great part of a new and better world, with the barbarian island of Ireland at the earth's end as foundation stone.

For a space, we leave him in the island monastery, and he even yet unaware of his great purpose.

CHAPTER III

"The Voice of the Irish"

1. MONKS OF THE WEST

The urban civilisation of the empire, rotten with luxury, was sensuous, worldly, and superstitious, like that now around us. Then, as now, devout souls found the world so much out of harmony with the spiritual life that they were driven to extreme austerity. Chesterton well says[1] of the people of the empire that "it was no metaphor to say that these people needed a new heaven and a new earth; for they had really defiled their own earth and even their own heaven. How could their case be met by looking at the sky, when erotic legends were scrawled in stars across it; how could they learn anything from the love of birds and flowers after the sort of love stories that were told of them?... Nothing could purge this obsession but a religion that was literally unearthly.... They had to go into the desert where they could find no flowers or even into the cavern where they could see no stars. Into that desert and that cavern the highest human intellect entered for centuries; and it was the very wisest thing it could do." In other words, monasticism was needed to purge the mind of man; and not until the days

---

1.   G. K. Chesterton, *St. Francis of Assisi.*

of St. Francis of Assisi, eight hundred years later, was the mental atmosphere of the imperial lands sweet. In the West, St. Ambrose encouraged monasticism at Milan, where St. Jerome spent his first years as a monk before going from busy Rome to Bethlehem, where he founded religious houses for both monks and nuns. Moved by the example of Ambrose, St. Augustine introduced monasticism in his African diocese.

Meanwhile, in Gaul, St. Martin had founded religious houses and monasticism had thriven so remarkably that the monks who attended his funeral, about the year 397, numbered two thousand. From Bethlehem, John Cassian brought the same ideal to Marseilles, where he founded the monastery of St. Victor in 412; and almost simultaneously St. Honoratus set up the most famous of the Gallic monasteries at Lérins, that pleasant island off Cannes, where now the Riviera holiday makers roar through the spray in speed-boats, but then disciples of the saint lived in the manner of the cenobites of Egypt. "Each monk had his own cell, where he lived and slept; but all met together for the Mass and the hours of the Divine Office; possibly also for meals. At some distance from the main group of cells, but within the islet (or in the neighbouring island of Lero) some of the more elderly and virtuous brethren lived as hermits.[2]

Tírechán, the very earliest biographer of Patrick, writing two centuries after the saint's death and quoting good authority, says that Patrick spent seven years travelling in Gaul, all Italy, and the Mediterranean islands; he says that Patrick visited Lérins. It seems plausible, even certain, that he grew familiar with the example of the great missionary monk St. Martin, that he made acquaintance

2.   John Ryan, S.J., *Irish Monasticism.*

with the community that St. Ambrose had founded at Milan. He would seek out the house of Ambrose as naturally as, in the days after St. Bernard, a questing soul inevitably would seek out Clairvaux. That he should enter on the monastic life at Lérins was but to do as many others, subsequently eminent like himself, did—St. Hilary, St. Caesarius, St. Lupus, St. Eucharius. "Whosoever craved for Christ, sought Honoratus," one of these saints said of his master.

We mark, therefore, the monastic spirit in which Patricius apprenticed to the work that he was to undertake. He was not ordained priest. In those days, most monks were laymen, in the West as well as the East; clerics among the monks were exceptions. We conceive the young monk, then, pacing the strand of Lérins, in rapt meditation, wondering and waiting for his mission.

2. The Call

At length—seven years after his flight from Antrim, and thirteen years after his seizure by the Irish raiders—Patricius left Lérins for Britain, to return to his own folk. They received him "as a son" (*ut filium susceperunt*), he says, so that it appears that his father and mother were dead, but other elders lived. Earnestly, he says, these good folk pleaded with the young monk, after so many tribulations, never to leave them again. He stayed some years; for his call had not come.

One night he dreamed, and his dream was a vision that came with the power of the Voice which he had heard on Slemish, years before. He knew that this was no vain fancy, but a message that he must obey. In his vision, he saw "a man coming as if from Ireland, whose name was Victorious, with very many letters." The man gave one of these letters to the dreamer, who read the beginning; namely, these words: *Vox Hyberionacum* (The Voice of the Irish).

Mark this strange expression. It was not the voice of the Ulstermen or the voice of the Picts or the voice of the men of Leinster that came to the dreamer, but the Voice of the Irish, the voice of a nation. It was so that Patrick, thought of the people of Ireland; they were a nation, a single community; they had a being, they were not a set of tribes. That island beyond the Roman world was then, what it never ceased to be, the territory and patrimony of a nationality, distinct and integral.

The dreamer began to read, and even as he read, he says, "I heard the voices of those who dwelt besides the wood of Focluth which is by the western sea; and thus they cried, as if with one mouth: 'We beseech thee, holy youth, to come and walk once more amongst us.'"

The "wood of Focluth" has not been identified, but it seems reasonable to think that it was the forest which stretched below Slemish to the Antrim coast. To Patrick, writing for readers in Britain, it would be natural to describe the Irish Channel as "the western sea"; to him in youth, and to all dwellers in Britain, the Irish channel was "the western sea" in fact and in name.

When he heard Irish voices calling to him in the dream, Patricius "was greatly touched in heart, and could read no more." He woke. Writing long afterwards, he adds: "Thanks be to God that after very many years the Lord granted to them according to their earnest cry."

Clearly, the love of Ireland moved him deeply. Nostalgia, such as the Irish exile knows well, was on him: the craving to return to a land and a life which have so strange a fascination. His days and nights on Slemish came to mind, no doubt: the Irish Spring, when the birds whistle through the moist air, over the freshening land; the changeful summer, glance and gleam; the mellow autumn, with broad suns setting beyond the heathery moor; the crisp winters and the Northern Lights that shake their yellow banners over the world, mysteriously—drifts of swans on Lough Neagh, strings of homing rooks across the plain, red trunks of the immemorial pine-woods, yew trees that seemed to have stood since creation beside untrodden beaches; the cry of the chase afar off, merry Irish children playing in the harvest fields: Ireland of the bluegreen distances and misty hills, brown bogs, dusted with snow, reek of the turf, goodly smell of farm, the friendly animals—all this, so different from the urbane Roman things, would come back like a spell. Most of all, there was compassion for the people, those country folk so rich in manly virtue, in hospitality and friendliness, and the gallant Fenian youths, with the dark hair starting from their brows like black flame while the grey eyes beneath seemed to be coloured by much gazing on a hunter's skies—these folk Patricius loved. They had captured him, they had enslaved him, but he knew them and liked them better than the city folk of the empire; he grieved that they lacked the supernatural life that glowed so abundantly in his saint's heart.

On another night, as he yearned for Ireland's people, a revelation came to him, which he describes in terms that show how far he had advanced in mystical union with God:

And on another night, whether within or beside me I know not, God knoweth, in the clearest words, which I heard but could not understand until the end of the prayer, He spoke out thus: "He who laid down His life for thee, He it is who speaketh within thee."

With joy, Patricius woke, he tells, and yet again he dreamed:

> And once more I saw Him praying in me and He was as
> it were within my body; and I heard him over me, that
> is over the interior man; and there strongly He prayed
> with groanings. And meanwhile I was astonished and
> marvelled, and considered who it was who prayed
> within me; but at the end of the prayer He spoke out to
> the effect that He was the Spirit.
>
> And so I awoke and remembered the Apostle saying:
> "The Spirit helpeth the infirmities of our prayer. For we
> know not what we should pray for as we ought; but the
> Spirit Himself asketh for us with unspeakable groanings
> which cannot be uttered in words." And again: "The
> Lord our advocate maketh intercession for us."

Let those who understand what the mystics, like Santa Teresa
and St. John of the Cross, say about the prayer of union, interpret
these sentences of our saint, as he describes the almost indescrib-
able; that is, the union of his soul and intentions with the Holy
Spirit, as he prayed for Ireland, having heard in a dream her people's voice.

"Towards Ireland of my own accord," he goes on, "I made no
move until I was almost worn out."

Thus, then, did the Apostle of Ireland receive his vocation.
Thus did he realise his purpose, to bring the faith to the enemies
that he had learnt to love. It was a conception that never could
come from himself, an ambition which an unscholarly ex-slave
never would discover for himself. The land which the Caesars had
not conquered, this youth was to evangelise and transform; but the

impulse came in those interior communications of the soul with
God.

3. THE TRAIL

Patricius left his people and his native land, and went to the Continent to prepare for the missionary life. He seems to have pur-
posed to go to Rome, to seek his training and ordination, and we
think of him as the forerunner of Irishmen of later times who went
overseas to seek armies to liberate Ireland; men like Patrick Sars-
field, whom the poet described as *Ag déanamh a ghearáin leis na
righthibh*—"pleading and pleading with the kings of the world."
Could the monk and mystic so prevail with the churchmen of the
troubled, trembling Roman world, as to gain the commission that
he craved?

On the road to Rome, he naturally would pass through Auxerre; but, coming to Auxerre, he stayed there. This city of Gaul was
a great centre of learning and piety, probably the greatest in the
West at that time. There Patricius, it is thought, was ordained deacon by the Bishop, St. Amator; he now began ten years of religious
life, study, and training. The Scriptures were his chief, if not his
only, literature. His mind became so saturated with Holy Writ that
in after days his utterances were full of Biblical diction. Nothing
less sublime, less spiritual, suited that practical mystic. The age
was one, like our own, when "highbrows" abounded, men who
loved words more than thoughts and language more than meaning. These *dilettanti* of the fifth century, when the world was being
remade by men like Patrick, scorned him for his lack of elegant
phrases and futile grammar. They thought more of a vague style,

the flowers of decay, than of vital language that comes from action; they wrote their *Hisperica Famina*, worthless poetry of the sort that we call "futurist," while he, in crude and virile words, composed an immortal *Confession*. He never overcame what he called *rusticitas*; that is, a blunt, unscholarly simplicity. Torn from a Latin-speaking home in boyhood, and spending his impressionable teens in a land of foreign speech, he never could become a cultivated speaker or writer. Little he cared.

For ten years, he awaited his next message from beyond the world. The year 429, when Patricius was aged about 45, was the year when the event took place which was to open the road to the achievement of his desire—*votum animae meae*, in his own phrase.

A British monk named Pelagius, living in Rome at the beginning of the century, had developed an heretical doctrine which appealed to many minds in that disordered age. He taught that man can win salvation by strength of character, without the aid of grace; that Christ's action on the soul is by example only. Where pride was strong, men liked to believe in their self-sufficiency, and what amounted to a false, naturalistic, and puritanical religion was preached by this dynamic man, aided by vehement disciples, of whom the chief was Caelestius, said to be Irish. After the fall of Rome, Pelagius and Caelestius fled to Africa, where St. Augustine rose in righteous indignation to refute the doctrine that denied the efficacy of grace. In the Holy Land, where Pelagius carried his subversive movement, St. Jerome in turn wrote vigorously against the heretics, describing one of them (presumably Caelestius) as "this most stupid fellow, heavy with Irish porridge." The heretical leaders were excommunicated in 417, and soon afterwards disappeared, but their doctrine continued to find followers in Gaul and Britain, where even some bishops clung to the condemned teaching. In the year 429, a synod in Troyes purified the Gallic Church. The Bishop of Auxerre now was St. Germanus, who had succeeded St. Amator some ten years earlier. This remarkable Gallic Churchman, a huntsman, a statesman, even a warrior, in turn, was the strongest figure in Gaul, and was selected by Pope St. Celestine to go into Britain to grapple with the heresy in the heretic's native land. With Germanus was sent St. Lupus of Lérins, formerly a fellow monk with Patrick.

Germanus met the leaders of Pelagianism in a conference at Verulamium (now St. Alban's), where discussion ended in the triumph of orthodoxy. The heretics were overcome, or submitted, and then the Gallic churchmen went through the land preaching in open places, and evoking a spiritual revival. With Britain restored to the pure faith and with zeal abounding, it was natural that the state of the neighbouring island was discussed. According to one fragment of evidence, Christians already living in Ireland sent an appeal to Rome, about this time, for a bishop to be sent to them. Perhaps they conveyed this appeal through Germanus; for the mission in Britain would come to their knowledge, and a messenger easily could be sent across the Channel. Furthermore, if it be true that Caelestius was Irish—and some have believed that Pelagius himself was an Irishman, either by birth or by blood—there would be strong reason to wish to establish orthodoxy across the Irish Sea.

At any rate, on one ground or another the scheme so dear to Patricius was debated, and our saint's dearest friend, now nameless, urged his appointment as leader of the proposed mission. "At home in Auxerre we have one who has lived in Ireland, knows the people and the language, and is full of the matter," that friend could argue.

"He fought for me in my absence," Patrick tells us. This nameless friend championed the rustic monk and won approval for him; so that, returning to Auxerre, he said to Patricius with his own lips, "Lo, thou art to be raised to the rank of bishop," telling him that he was to lead the mission to Ireland, in accordance with his cherished dream.

High rose the hopes of our saint; yet, even in the hour of his exultation, the greatest trial of his life came. A conference was held at Auxerre in 430 to go fully into the scheme. The Gallic Church would be required to finance the undertaking, and there were many to satisfy. He who led the expedition must be a bishop, but there were those, among the scholarly Gauls, who thought the ex-slave unfitted for the episcopal dignity. Accordingly, the claims of the enthusiast wavered in the balance; and now it was that the very man who had proposed Patricius turned the scale against him.

How can we explain this strange and deplorable act? We know the type of character, ardent and inconstant, that is capable of such whims. The friend of our saint spoke words that galled Patrick to his life's end.

In some intimate talk, Patrick once had told this brother in religion of a sin that he had committed in boyhood—something that he "had done one day, nay in one hour," before he was fifteen years old, and before he had grown strong in virtue or acquired the faith that came to him in his years of trial. This fault Patricius had disclosed through a scruple before he received the diaconate, ten years earlier; and now the friend to whom he had imparted the secret disclosed it to his superiors.

We may suppose that the fault was one of presumption—some youthful, ambitious boast, perhaps—for manifestly it was something that seemed incompatible with the desire for leadership of a mission. Suppose that it was said: "This Patricius, who now asks your reverences to entrust him with high responsibility, boasted in youth that he would be a great man; he is proud and arrogant, on his own admission." Suspicion of a fault of this kind is just that which would destroy the hopes which Patrick cherished in all humility. However that may be, the false friend's disclosure did result both in the disappointment of the would-be missionary and in his public humiliation.

The soul was so wounded that the thing rankled thirty years afterwards; for the aged bishop wrote at length about it in his *apologia*, telling how "certain my elders came and urged my sins against my laborious episcopate"—that is, his faults against his readiness for a toilsome vocation. He was near to despair. He dreamed, and saw a writing that dishonoured him, and heard a divine voice which spoke of the bishop-designate despoiled of his calling. "Truly," says Patrick, "in that day I was strongly pushed that I might fall here and for ever"—he was near to despair. What a trial was this! Always Patrick seems to have been acutely sensitive, a consequence of much loneliness, no doubt. The years that he had spent shut off from his friends, driven in youth to make decisions for himself, dwelling with no earthly counsel but his own, had made him conscious of a difference with the well-educated men among whom he moved. Little his friends knew of his interior anguish, his watchings, temptations, wrestlings with misfortune, mighty acts of faith. To be judged by these as an ignorant fellow and presumptuous, and to lose his bishopric just as it was promised to him—this was torment to his gentle spirit, and for a space he stared into the gulf of despair that is around all men, ready to receive the losers of faith and hope. He did not fall into that spiritual abyss; he persevered. "The Lord," he writes, "graciously had

pity on the stranger and sojourner for His name's sake, and He
helped me greatly in that humiliation, so that I did not utterly fall
into disgrace and reproach."

4. The Pope's Choice

At that time, then, the candidature of Patrick was rejected. He was
left to his religious duties at Auxerre, while the commission was
given to another. A Roman churchman, St. Palladius, had advised
Pope Celestine to send the late Gallic mission into Britain, and now
St. Celestine, presumably on the advice of Germanus, selected Palladius for the work in Ireland. This chapter of our story is studded
with the names of saints. He whom we now name was a Roman
by birth, had lived with St. Ambrose at Milan, and was the dear
friend of St. Augustine. He ruled the Church in a turbulent pontificate, and was the crusher of Nestorian heresy. His last great act was
the commission to his deacon, St. Palladius, whom he consecrated
bishop in 431, and sent "to the Scots believing in Christ, as their
first bishop."

It is needless, of course, to explain that the term Scots signified
the Irish in that age, and down to the thirteenth century. Some
explanation is needed, however, of the terms of the missionary
bishop's undertaking. He was sent, according to these terms, not
to the pagans of Ireland to convert them, but to Christians already
living in the country, to organise them as members of the Catholic Body. From this, we perceive in the first place that there were
sufficient Christians in Ireland to call for an organised Church.
We perceive in the second place that the mission of Palladius was
on a different scale from that which Patrick had conceived when,

with a soul that groaned with the desire of God to whom he was united, he embraced the pagan Irish of his captivity in his love and yearned to gather all into the arms of the Church. Perhaps, the great churchmen of Gaul and Rome so regarded the strange race beyond the Roman world—a race of whom fabulous stories of cannibalism were believed by St. Jerome himself (as we learn from his writings)—perhaps, we say, those churchmen regarded the barbarians overseas as a race too sadly reprobate for the immediate conversion to which the monk Patricius looked with such sanguine hope. A more modest achievement was to be undertaken; and he, the Irish speaker, was not even taken as a member of the mission. It is easy to conceive the mortification with which he saw the bishop from Rome set out. This was his dark hour; but his resignation to the Divine will was soon to earn a surprising recompense.

To whom did Palladius go? Who were the Christians then living in Ireland? It is not possible to answer with assurance, but we know that considerable intercourse went on between Irish ports and the Continent—at one time, as record tells, the ports of Ireland were better known to the classical world than those of Britain—and it is easy to conceive how traders and others on the southern Irish coast had come to share the faith of Christendom, and doubtless had some proficiency in Latin, the *lingua franca* of the Roman world. On the Continent, there are records of several churchmen of note who were born in Ireland; for example, Mansuetus, Bishop of Toul about 350. These doubtless were firstlings of the faith in Ireland—souls that believed, and went to already Christian lands in order to enter upon the full Christian life.

Little, isolated Christian communities grew up here and there and gave saints to Ireland and heaven. Besides native Christians like these, there were Gallic settlers who sought refuge in Ireland from the turmoil of the Continent. It is held by some scholars that the migration of scholars from Gaul early in the fifth century amounted to an exodus, and that these settlers were the founders of Ireland's classical learning, which was so conspicuous in the following age. If we accept the theory of large-scale Gallic settlements, swelling the meagre Christian population in the coastal region looking towards the Continent, the character of the mission of Palladius, as one to people already half Continental in speech and mind, becomes yet clearer.

Within a year of Palladius' setting forth to Ireland, he was dead in Britain. Commonly, it is assumed that his mission was a failure. The records are scanty. The bishop and his few priests landed at Wicklow, and are said to have been received unfavourably by the rulers, or by Druids; but three churches were founded. Tigroney (Co. Wicklow) commemorates the work of Palladius to this day; for the name means Roman House, *Teach-na-Róm-hdánach*. At Donard and Dunlavin, lovely places in the lower highlands of Wicklow, are other sites that Palladius consecrated. From Ireland, Palladius went to Britain, where death overtook him; the reason for his departure from the mission field is not known. The assumption that he failed and fled is facile, but surely foolish. Would a great churchman from the capital of Christendom, after undertaking a work, abandon it in a few months? To organise three communities in that time, when a mere survey of the ground would be work enough, does not look like failure. Surely it is more reasonable to believe that Palladius, once in the mission field, found the harvest so abundant, so ripe for the reapers, that he recognised the insufficiency of himself and his staff for all that was to be done. Not the few Christians already living in the southeastern district and able to discourse with Latin-speaking clergy, were the harvest, but the innumerable souls of the population. These barbarians, seen in their own land, were no savages. They were kindly, they had a vigorous native culture, they were manly and possessed of high natural qualities; Ireland was true mission ground, and the ideas of the monk Patricius were sound. Therefore Palladius resolved to lay what he had found in his survey before his superiors; that is, before Germanus, in whose charge the mission country lay. The journey to Britain was made on the way to Gaul, which the missionary never reached. One account says that he was attacked on British soil and martyred.

Is not this the most plausible reading of the brevity of Palladius' mission? It is borne out by the immediate decision of the authorities. When Palladius died, Patrick already was on his way to join the mission—perhaps, the Irish-speaker had been summoned by the bishop. Messengers bringing news of the bishop's death met Patrick's party at a place in Gaul thought to be Evreux, and all returned to Auxerre. There was little doubt now what ought to be done. Patrick, who had been rejected in 431, was consecrated bishop by the Pope's desire a few days before St. Celestine died in July 432, and, in the autumn, commissioned by Germanus on the Pope's authority, at last sailed for Ireland, on that work for which he had been prepared in such manifestly providential ways.

CHAPTER IV

The Winter at Saul

1. THE VOYAGE

The expedition which sailed from Gaul numbered twenty-five persons, according to one of the oldest accounts. The Bishop Patricius had with him priests, some Gallic, some British, with artificers and others necessary to the work of a mission in the field of action.

Where Palladius had come ashore—the estuary, called Inver Dea, just north of the Wicklow Head, which lies like an illuminated map of golden sand, blue water, and black-green forest, beneath the view of whosoever crosses the road from Rathnew southward—here, in country that seems to be filled with heaven's own peace, the vessel came ashore. Sad to say, the mission was ill received, like that of Palladius in the previous year. Fishermen who were netting the inver refused to supply the Christians, and soon the chieftain of the district, one Nathi mac Garrchon, came with his followers and violently drove them back to sea. One of Patrick's disciples had his teeth knocked out. This sufferer for the cause is commemorated now by the very name of Wicklow, in Irish, i.e., *Cill Manntain*, the Church of Manntan, the Toothless One. Northward the expedition cruised some forty miles, to anchor in Inver Domhrann, the shallow, sand Bay of Malahide. A visit was made to a little island, now called Holmpatrick, Inispatrick, or St. Patrick's Island; and so much was this spot revered in later days, because the national Apostle once touched upon it, that a monastic house was founded there; this was the meeting place of a national Synod centuries later. The estuary of the river now called the Nanny, north of Skerries, also was visited, in search of provisions, "but nothing was found for him there"—the island he had come to bless was strangely inhospitable to the Apostle. Perhaps this decided Patrick to make for Ulster, the region that he knew, and where he could be sure of making friendly contacts.

Another visit ashore was more fortunate. Somewhere near the Delvin river (which now forms the boundary between the counties of Dublin and Meath) the Christian party went ashore. There, where the green land slopes to a wide, smooth strand and the eyes behold the mountains of Ulster along the sea horizon to the north, they rested, and the travel-weary Bishop slept. A gentle youth, the son of a man of that country named Sescneu, wandering there, came upon the party, and gathered flowers and laid them in the bosom of the sleeping cleric, as some sort of loving homage to one whom he recognised as worthy of tribute.

"Do not do that," said one of the Christians, "lest the Bishop wake."

The story says that Patrick woke; and, seeing the lad with the flowers and marking what he had done, said:

"Trouble him not; he will be my heir."

The lad was Benen, whom we call St. Benignus. He entered the apostle's service, became his devoted attendant, and at length his assistant bishop in the Primacy.

One narrative says that Patrick founded there his first church, and left two of his clerics in charge of it. He went next, it is said, to the estuary of the Boyne, where he rested a while and blessed the place; but some think that this is a mistake by an early writer who confused the Boyne with the Delvin. Whether from the Delvin or the Boyne, the next stage of the voyage was the last. Standing out from the vast, shallow bay of Dundalk, the vessel sailed past the coloured hills of Cooley and the mouth of Carlingford Lough, and so went by the sublime mountains of Mourne, then growing red with the withering of the bracken, on and on, along the Ulster coast, past the gentle shore of Lecale to Inver Brenea—the mouth of Strangford Lough. This is the most dangerous stretch of water that the vessel met on the voyage.

Strangford Lough is the later, Norse-given name, of what Patrick knew as Loch Cuan, a sea-lough eighteen miles long and five wide; it opens on the sea by a long winding channel, in width about one mile. Thus, with every tide, about a hundred square miles of salt water are driven out, or sucked back, through a funnel of land—Lecale of Down to the one hand, the Ards Peninsula to the other. Roaring and rushing and foaming, millions of tons of water are hurled to and fro, making a cauldron of difficulty, even in the fairest weather. Far out to sea the disturbance is felt, so that yachtsmen of today set a course almost out of sight of land when they wish to pass the mouth of this fierce sea-lough. Only the brave and well-experienced venture to enter the mouth and the channel, to navigate the inrushing torrent like surf-riders, up between the green and wooded shores, on swift and swirling eddies, an eight-mile perilous course to where Portaferry's white walls and custering masts mark a little harbour on the right hand. Portaferry—*Port-na-Peireadh*—is aptly named; the Irish means the Port of Squalls.

2. THE LANDING

This most difficult channel, the Gallic boat passed. How was it done without a local pilot? Was it the apostle's intrepid faith that led him to cast his life and his cause upon the waters of the north? Seeing that this part of Ulster was strange to Patrick, can it be that his purpose had been to fare on, past Down and Belfast Lough to the Antrim coast that he knew, and that storm or exhaustion overtook him, after the eighty-mile voyage from the Meath shore, so that he cast the boat upon the inward rushing tide as a last chance of survival? At least, there is no doubt that the desperate passage was made. The place where the ship came ashore is named in ancient record and pointed out by tradition. It is Inver Slane, or the mouth of the Slane stream, on the other side of the water from Portaferry and several miles farther on. In this little estuary, the Gallic craft was hidden, the records tell, and the clerics went ashore to rest. The stress laid on their exhaustion seems to confirm our guess that the venture into Loch Cuan was made as a desperate cast, driven by storm from the sea, or by hunger or thirst. The party was in utterly strange surroundings—neither in the Antrim that the Bishop knew, nor on the Leinster coast where Christians were not unfamiliar. The path that the clerics followed from Ringbane on the Slaney stream to the place that we call Saul is still seen. They rested in a barn, and there they were found by the swineherd of Dichu, the lord of that place. Taking the travel-worn strangers for robbers, the servant went to his master, who came with his dog to drive the clerics forth.

Then Patrick chanted the prophetic verse, *Ne tradas, Domine, bestiis animas confidentes tibi* (the ancient narrative says), and the dog became silent.

Patrick had old familiarity with Irish hounds, and he easily quelled the beast, no doubt.

Dichu, when he saw the Bishop, was seized with grief, we are told. Here is one more example of the saint winning hearts by his very appearance; goodness and command were in his bearing, it seems, and folk of goodwill were converted by his saintliness. Dichu "believed, and Patrick baptised him; so that he is the first who received in Ulster baptism and belief from Patrick."[1] The old narrative makes the belief and baptism seem to be instantaneous; but we may assume a spell of time, perhaps of months, seeing that the mission wintered at that place.

The barn where the Christian voyagers had rested was given to Patrick, and he made it his first church in Ulster. Hence Saul, from *sabhall*, a barn, is the name of that place in Lecale where the conversion of Ireland began, to this day. In the Catholic church at Saul, Patrick's altarstone is preserved, and we may unite ourselves tangibly with the marvellous time when, in the mornings of the Ulster winter, between the golden candlelights, the saint offered his first Masses in Ireland for the enterprise that made us, fifty generations later, still children of the Church of God. Over Saul there rises a steep hill which commands sublime views of the north—the lough with its hundreds of tree-clad isles like floating baskets of flowers, the sea beyond the foaming channel away to the grey cloud which is the Isle of Man, the peaks of stately Mourne beyond Lecale's kindly farming land; the twisted stone walls about little fields far inland; the smoke-cloud over Belfast far away, a glint of the water-plain of Lough Neagh through mists of distance. From this eminence, Patrick must have viewed and

---

1.   *Tripartite Life.*

loved our Ulster, as we do; and he still does so, in an immense stone effigy.

In 1932, the fifteenth centenary of the saint's coming, the foundation was laid here of a national memorial to Patrick. In 1938, it was dedicated by the Cardinal Primate, Patrick's successor. Today the gigantic granite figure, vested and holding the shamrock which is Patrick's symbol, dominates the far-extending scene, a landmark to a vast region, and a symbol of the constant devotion of the race.

Providential, assuredly, was that decision which brought the mission into Ireland by the perilous water-gate, hither, to good Dichu's countryside. Patrick's words are recorded, and we repeat them—

> *God's blessing on Dichu*
> *Who gave me the Barn!*
> *May he have afterwards*
> *A heavenly home, bright, pure, great!*

3. Miliuc's Children

We have said that the mission wintered at Saul. Of the work of the winter months we have no record, but a legend says that Patrick journeyed to Slemish—a distance of some thirty-five miles— to visit his old master, Miliuc; that the children of Miliuc who had been his playmates and now were of middle age like himself accepted the faith, but that Miliuc himself refused conversion, shut himself in his house, fired it, and perished.

It may well be true that the old playmates of "Cothrige" were touched by his return as a great cleric, seeking them out to renew his friendship, and that their love of the saintly boy made them ready converts of the Bishop; but the supposed suicide of their father is one of those extravagant touches with which the legends of Patrick teem, and which we instinctively prune away as we seek probability. The stubborn pagan was described, perhaps, in some fiery oratorical phrase, and a legend grew. Perhaps, Miliuc's refusal was due to a pride, which would not accept salvation from one who had been slave, at the master's beck and call.

At length, the Lent of the year 433 came round, and now our story becomes eventful—pregnant with great deeds.

CHAPTER V

The Fires of Slan

1. MEATH'S FIRST CHRISTIANS

One day in Lent, a boat sailed up the winding reaches of the Boyne, past the battlefields and the monstrous *tumuli* on the north bank which are the burial mounds of kings who died when Pharoahs were buried under Pyramids in Egypt, past Slane's steep, verdant hill, and on by sluggish winding reaches towards *An Uaimh*, or Navan. When the rough leather sail got no helping wind, the men in the craft would scull.

It was a pleasant trip, between grassy banks where trees were growing faintly green above bushes of golden whin, the glory of the Irish Spring; a trip of twenty miles. The river-voyagers must have camped somewhere on the river banks for a night; for it was early morning when they arrived at the Ford of the Alders, Trim. There, where the river sweeps like silver light round pastures, the little boat came ashore. On a low eminence, not far from the water, was a rampart that surrounded a sunny house, from which the inmates watched with curious eyes.

The chief of the travellers, having landed, read in a holy book. A lad came running from the house to interrupt the traveller's devotion.

"Who are you, stranger?" the boy asked.

"I am Lommán, a priest, of the company of Patricius the Bishop,"
was the answer, spoken in learner's Gaelic.

"Are you a Briton, holy sir?"

"I am."

"My mother is a Briton," the boy said. "She has named me Fort-
chearn, which the British call Vortigern."

"And your father, my lad?"

"He is Felim, the son of the High-King. Come, my mother will
make you welcome."

Lommán had found the household that he was seeking. He
was welcomed in the language of the Britons, the Celtic speech
that had P's instead of K's.

Felim's wife had known the faith in Britain, and doubtless she
had prepared her husband and son for it. Glad she was to welcome a priest to that house beside the Boyne. Lommán baptised
the household, and the parents committed their boy to him to be
reared for the Church. House and land at Trim were made over to
the mission.

When these good folk enquired how the Bishop, Patricius, was
faring, since he landed with his twenty-four helpers last autumn,
Lommán would have surprising news: "He is in Meath already."

He would tell how Patricius had spent the winter in Ulster,
the clerics copying missals and the craftsmen making crosses and
vestments; and how, when the Spring came, and all was ready, the
Gallic ship had been launched again and steered out through the
raging channel of the sea-loch, and had sailed past the mountains
of Mourne and along Louth's low coast to the Boyne's mouth. Here
Patricius had bade the pilot steer up the river mouth to a reedy
landing place near Mornington (as the spot is called now), and had
come ashore in Royal Meath, the province which was the mensal

land of the monarchs of Ireland. One Cianán of Duleek, a Christian, is said to have brought Patrick to this place; and it is suggested that Cianán was an Irish Christian who returned to his native land from the Continent or Britain, with the mission.

"And now," Lommán would say, "the Bishop waits at the Boyne's mouth to advance to Tara, that he may preach the faith before the High-King himself, and win permission to establish the Church in Ireland. He has sent me to take counsel with you, whom he knew to be his friends."

There was a conference of those first Christians of Meath, and the next move of the mission seems to have been made in the light of the counsel taken at Trim; the mission was to move to Slane and to celebrate Easter on that high hill by the Boyne, which looked over the High-King's territory.

2. THE BISHOP AT SLANE

At Slane, the Bishop and his helpers set up their mission station. Mass was said, very likely, under a shieling, and the first Christians of Meath may have come in during Holy Week to receive the sacraments from the Bishop of the Irish himself.

Patrick probably sat *in praetorio* then, on the hill which commands all the blue distances of Meath, as he conferred with his people and his converts. To our eyes, he would appear to be wearing ecclesiastical vestments; for the vestments of today are much what the habitual dress of Roman citizens of good position was in his time. He was clean shaven in the Roman manner, unlike the moustached and bearded Irish; his crown was tonsured, and he wore the soft, dented cap, which developed into the mitre. He bore a staff which was altogether remarkable. For centuries afterwards it was revered as the *Bachall Iosa*, the Baculum of Jesus, and the place in which it was preserved is named Ballyboghil, the Town of the Baculum, to this day. This staff was believed to have been carried once by our Blessed Lord Himself, who was crucified and rose again just 400 years before that Easter at Slane. It was borne by Patrick as a relic of the utmost sanctity. Whether the story of its origin was true or only legendary, the fact that Patrick used it in his missionary travels would suffice, surely, to make it venerable in later times. Conceive, then, the meaning of its end. In the sixteenth century, when an English prelate was sent to Dublin as King Henry the Eighth's archbishop, the relic venerated since Patrick's day in Ireland was taken from the place of its custody and burnt in the street by that alien prelate, in hatred for all that it signified, whether legendary or authentic.

Another relic of Patrick's mission escaped the reforming destroyers. That was his Mass bell, which we still possess. It is made of hammered iron, roughly, as if by a village blacksmith, riveted, and coated with bronze. Including the handle, it is less than eight inches high. There is no clapper. It is sounded, as the many other old Irish bells were, by being struck. In the eleventh century, the high age of Irish culture, the coarse, old bell was enshrined reverently in a case of bronze, silver, and gold, with precious stones and magnificent interlacing ornament in the style called Celtic. "The beauty, richness, and intricacy of the workmanship of the shrine," writes a Scottish antiquary, "discloses to us the taste and skill prevailing at the time, and indicate the degree of veneration for the rude object of hammered iron to which so magnificent a work of art was given as a covering." Our generation heard that bell ring, fifteen hundred years after the coming of Patrick; for it was struck at the Mass in

Phoenix Park in 1932, when a million worshippers attended the Eucharistic Congress; and, a few hours later, at Benediction in the heart of the Irish capital.

The Bishop, we have said, took counsel with the Christians of Meath, there on Slane hill. They would counsel him not to venture to Tara for the present. "There is danger, Lord Bishop, at this season."

"How so?" Patricius would ask, but he was resolved to go.

"Go not," the native advisers would say, "for this is the time of the fiery festival of the Spring, which the Magi of the heathen hold on the royal hill."

Perhaps it was the newly baptised prince, Felim, whose garment bore in its edges the Seven Colours of Nobility to denote his royal rank—perhaps it was he who gave reasons for not advancing on Tara.

On the day that we count March 25, the High-King's people would keep the birthday of the year, the fiery feast of Spring. On the eve, no fire must be seen in all the country, until the ceremonial fire of Spring was lighted, in the High-King's presence, on Tara hill. Then there would be a heathen festival, with hymns chanted to the morrow's sun—the sun, that fire in the sky which is the father of all fires; "and fire, the Druids say," the prince would explain, "is that by which all things live."

"The day you name," the Bishop would answer, "will be that day which we call the Lord's day, *Dominica*, which in Irish is *Dia Domhnaigh*."

The Irish would repeat the words, *Dia Domhnaigh*.

"Moreover," the Bishop would continue, "the coming Lord's Day will be Paschal Sunday, *Domhnach Cásca*."

Mark how the Latin Pasch, by the P-into-K rule, became *Cáisc*, *Cásca*, when it was made Gaelic. In the year 432, Easter Sunday fell on March 25, a coincidence of the Christian festival with the pagan day of observance which was truly dramatic: for from that coincidence sprang the conflict and the challenge.

"There is no better day for my task," Patrick must have said. "I will announce my mission by lighting the Paschal Fire at this place on Easter Eve!"

That is what he did. Meanwhile, there was a remarkable work to be done, that Holy Saturday. On Slane Hill, the Bishop ordained Cianân of Duleek, whom we venerate as a saint.

3. Challenge to Tara

He was always intrepid, that Bishop Patricius, called the Shaveling by those bearded Irish folk who were against him. Nothing that his friends could say would turn him from his purpose. As he had run away from slavery in boyhood, at the call of an inner voice, so now he was resolved to challenge all the powers of the Druids. He was not content to kindle a little fire at the mission station, as he directed the ceremonies that Holy Saturday in 433; but he directed that a vast beacon should be fired with the blessed flame.

His courage roused courage in those around him. With what high passion of hope they saw the golden fire blaze suddenly, through the dark March night, into a flaming column, or a soaring banner of light rushing up with a roar over the darkened land! It was a challenge more daring than that of any beacon of war; they knew it, those unarmed few by the tents and the shieling and the roughly shaped cross, on Slane hill.

At Tara, all was dark. The heart of the vast banqueting hall was a black cavern, and its high timbers creaked in the night air.

Windows in the raths of the Kings and the hostages and the Druids, were blind. Guided by lime-whitened stones that glimmered in the night, a little procession came to the ceremonial place on one high mound, where brushwood was heaped.

These were the High-King Laoghaire, and certain of the minor Kings, with the white-robed Druids: they chanted as they went some hymn in praise of the Natural forces—poetry such as a druid of our own days[1] has made:

> O earth, enchantress, mother, to our home
> > In thee we press,
> Thrilled by the fiery breath and wrapt in some
> > Vast tenderness....
> But gather ye, to whose undarkened eyes
> > Night is as day,
> Leap forth, immortals, birds of paradise,
> > In bright array,
> Robed like the shining tresses of the sun
> > by his name,
> Call from his haunt divine the ancient one
> > Our father flame!

Whether it was some Druid or the High-King himself who, with tinder, was to waken fire from darkness and ignite that beacon on the royal hill, we know not. Most likely it was the king—but before the pagan hands had struck the spark that would set the beacon ablaze, to give fire that would be distributed to every hearth and torch and turn Tara into a hill-city of light—to be a signal to

---

1. George W. Russell (A. E.), *Poems.*

every beacon-hill around, so that the royal land of Meath would
be illuminated and all folk would worship the fire and the light of
Spring: *That other beacon stabbed the northern sky!*

Even as hills are crowned at this season with the golden lines of
the whin-fires, as the country folk clear the moorlands of the great
golden weed to make rough grazing, so Slane Hill, ten miles distant
from Tara, swiftly glowed into light.

It was not the Druids, it was not the High-King, who had lit the
first flame of the Spring in hushed and darkened Meath! For the
first time in history some new, some strange authority had come
before the lords of Tara. There was amazement on the fireless royal
hill: but all knew where that fiery height to the north stood, and
some knew who had done that thing.

Had not the priests from the Roman land camped there on
Slane hill?

"Lord King!" some bearded Druid cried, uttering a warning
that has been remembered in tradition ever since, "that fire must
be quenched! He who lit it must be slain! If you let that fire burn
this night, it will burn forever in Eire!"

Again they said to the startled king, "He who lit that fire will
win all your people!"

"It shall not be," the king answered. "We will put these people
to death. Chariots!"

Then, through the plain of Meath, that was fragrant with the
smell of ploughed fields and rising sap, nine chariots and many
horsemen rode forth, making for the flaming hill.

4. "Come You to Tara!"

Meanwhile, Patricius stood on the great height at Slane, where the beacon of golden light had driven upward through the late dusk of Easter Eve, and we can imagine how the young men among his helpers worked to keep the new fire blazing.

"Pile on the fuel, lads," one of them would cry, and the rest would drag more new-hewn wood as near as he could to that scorching furnace, and hurl it in.

No blaze showed on Tara. The men on Slane must have guessed that their act had thrown the Druids on the royal hill into doubt or confusion. Lights, however, gleaned out on hills farther afield, where, mistaking Patrick's flame for Tara's, watchers lit the answering beacons.

"Pile on more fuel!"

Then, above the roar of the fire, there sounded through the night a distant clatter of hooves and grinding of wheels on the flagged road. Torches tossed a wild light. Chariots were approaching.

Nine chariots brought the High-King of Ireland, his queen, two Druids and other notables; riders on horseback with them. Making a big leftward cast they had come, from Tara to Duleek, fording the Boyne at Old-bridge, and by the Slane road toward the fiery hill.

As the cavalcade drew near and shouts were heard, maybe some of the company at the camp on Slane hill were fearful, but not so the Bishop. Like a general when the battle that he has sought is joined, Patricius watched and waited and listened.

The royal party halted somewhere on the hill's side, perhaps where the church of today stands, not far from the crossroads. Laoghaire, in his royal robe, and wearing his crown, as Irish kings wore them before battle, would have sprung from his chariot and climbed the slope to that illuminated camp, but he was restrained.

"If you go to the Christian, you will surrender to him, Lord King," someone said. "Bid him come to you."

So a gilly was sent, clambering up the hill, to invite the strangers to the High-King's presence.

He was one of Ireland's greatest kings, this Laoghaire, son of Niall of the Captives—of that Niall who had plundered Britain. Unlike his father, he seldom went to war. He was a man of peace, and a fine statesman. What was happening in the Roman world he watched and studied. In those days, Theodosius the Younger, Emperor, was causing the laws of the Roman world to be codified. Laoghaire, in turn, caused the laws of the Irish world to be put in order: his lawyers compiled the Seanchas Mór, the great Code of Irish Law. Such was the king. Around him, at the halting place on Slane hill, his kneeling warriors made a wall of shields, and so he waited, sitting with his queen and his Druids.

On the night air rose the Latin chant, as the little company of missionary clergy drew near: "Some put their trust in chariot and some in horses; but we will walk in the name of the Lord our God."

Patricius walked behind his clerics, vested in his Roman garb, and bearing his sacred staff, and so the slave-boy whom Niall had captured came in majesty before Niall's son.

The calmness of this unarmed company, the high bearing of the Bishop, the mysterious beauty of the Roman chant, were strange and impressive. Within the wall of shields how many felt moved to rise, honouring the comers? One broke the command that none should rise; it was Erc mac Dega, a man of law. This lawyer stood and honoured Patricius; later, he was Bishop of Slane, and was buried at that place.

Of the talk between Patricius and Laoghaire, we have no clear record.

The Bishop seems to have said that he came to establish in Ireland the religion of the Blessed Trinity and the Christian Church. It is recorded that one of Laoghaire's Druids broke into angry blasphemy against the Triune God, and perished there—as it seems, in a fit of apoplectic fury. Perhaps his fury was despair; for the case was going against the pagans. This is clear from the queen's entreaty. She pleaded with the Bishop not to be angered with the king. Even then and there, Patricius had a moral ascendancy.

At the end of the talk, whatever was said, Laoghaire was overcome. Instead of compelling the Christians to stamp out that fire of theirs—which by now had set all the beacons of Meath blazing, doubtless—he gave Patrick his grand desire.

"Come you to Tara tomorrow," he said, "and we will hear you in our court."

The wall of shields was broken, the chariots and the horsemen turned back by the Boyne road for Tara. In the camp on the hill, Patricius and his company prepared for rest, while the fateful beacon sank into a red glow, its work done.

"Tomorrow, after the Paschal Mass," Patricius announced, "we will take the road and carry the Cross to Tara of the Kings"—and who can doubt that his voice trembled with joy and triumph? Aye, but there were some in Ireland who were not pleased with that night's work. Along the road to Tara, the angered Druids went, halting here and there to stir up the people and to lay ambushes for these invaders, who bore no sword.

CHAPTER VI

The Cross Enters Tara

1. The Deer's Cry

"Slay the Roman!" whispered certain of King Laoghaire's servants to folk who dwelt on the road between Slane and Tara. "The King will be pleased if the stranger never comes to the Hill of the Kings."

Some such hint was given by enemies of Patrick—Druids or others in the High-King's company, who hated the stranger and his cause. An ambush was prepared. Who were the agents of the plotters? Who was to strike the murderous blow? It is easy to suppose that they were old soldiers, those disbanded Fenians who had served Laoghaire's father, when Niall mustered his raiding armies to attack the Roman world, dwelling now at cross-road villages, perhaps. Such men, old scarred fighters with glibbed hair half hiding their fierce, hunters' eyes, would listen readily to some such incitement: "A Roman, one of that proud breed, has come to Ireland, to seek mastery here. That is the camp of his people that you saw away up on Slane hill, busy like a bee-skep in summer. The insolent one; his fires were lighted to insult the son of Niall, Laoghaire your King!"

Then, through the night, Laoghaire's servants would make their way to Tara, after the High-King's chariot, leaving the nets of wrath spread upon the way that Patricius must travel.

So Easter morning dawned, in that year 433; and, at Slane hill, the Bishop celebrated Mass at his mission altar under the shielding—the *scáthlán*, as the altar-huts were called in the Penal days; there are people still living who remember Mass said under a *scáthlán* in the churchless parts of Ulster. Britons and Gauls, and the newly ordained Cianán and the prince Felim and his family would be there, and folk of the countryside would kneel far off, watching this strange act of the Holy Sacrifice, dumbly sharing in it, and wondering. Then, when he had broken fast, Patricius took eight chief helpers and little Benignus, his *giolla*, who carried the Bishop's writing materials; and with that little company he set forth for Tara. At the head of the tiny procession, one carried the Cross, the *vexillum* of the spiritual conquest. It was Cianán who bore the wax-lights to be kindled later.

Some twelve Roman miles, *millia passuum circiter XII*, the journey was. Patricius would remember the road that he had walked twenty-six years earlier as a slave-boy in flight from the north.

The Boyne could be forded near Slane, or crossed in those coracles of skin which have been in use on the Boyne at all times, even down to living memory—there are a few still used by fishermen. Up from the ferry, the Christian company strode along the rising road, leaving Rossnaree below to the left hand, with the enormous *tumuli* on the north bank grandly visible. They would walk with the steady, rhythmic step that all travellers in the Roman land learnt from the legions; and so Patricius faced the dangers spread before him.

Behold him now, no tattered stripling in flight, but a man of mature middle age, dressed in white and corded linen and the *paenula* or chasuble of Roman rank, with gilt border and broad purple stripes. The Irish of his little company—Cianán and Benignus—are in native dress of kilted cloth.

Well he knows by the signs around him, when people draw within doors and avoid the highway as the little band goes onward through the green-gold land, that mischief has been prepared. He is wary-eyed, watching for some gathering to oppose him, to bar the way, to assault the weaponless nine. There is no fear in that holy heart of his, but he wishes to raise the courage of his followers, so he breaks into a marching anthem that he himself makes in the Irish tongue. We have the strange poem still, for, under the Gaelic title of *Faed Fiada*, the Deer's Cry, and the Latin title, St. Patrick's *Lorica* or Breastplate, it has been preserved and revered by every generation since his day.[1]

The Gaelic that we have runs to ten stanzas, with four Latin lines at the end. Probably, it is an elaboration, made in a later century, of the actual chant that was made on the road to Slane; nevertheless, much of it is almost certainly authentic:

I.

Atomriug indíu
Niurt trén togairm Trinoit,
Cretim Treodataid foísitin Oendatad,
In dúlemain dail.

II.

Atomriug indiu
Niurt Gene Crist co na Bathius,

---

1.   The *Lorica* is published in many works, and is even sung today in J. C. Mangan's translation. Consult Eleanor Knott, *Eriu* VII, 239.

Niurt Crochta co n-a Adnocul
Niurt n-Eseirge co Fresgabail,
Niurt Tónuid do Brethemnas Bratha....

The company would catch the rhythm and fall into the chant, and so the famous hymn would throb in manly voices through the land:

> *I take for my sureties today:*
> > *The Trinity and Unity of God,*
> > *The birth of Christ,*
> > *His baptism, crucifixion, burial,*
> > *His resurrection, ascension,*
> > *His coming to the judgment of doom.*

Perhaps this rhythmic Gaelic catalogue of things believed was made by Patrick in his lonely days on Slemish and later used by him to teach his converts the elementary Christian truths, even as that other mighty missionary, St. Francis Xavier, taught the faith in little chants in Eastern tongues. Wonderfully eloquent the simple catalogue becomes:

> *I take for my sureties today:*
> > *The power of the love of the Seraphim,*
> > *The obedience of Angels,*
> > *The service of Archangels,*
> > *The prayers of the noble Fathers,*
> > *The predictions of Prophets,*
> > *The preaching of Apostles,*
> > *The faith of Confessors,*

The purity of holy Virgins,
The acts of righteous men.

I take for my sureties:
    The power of God to guide me,
    The might of God to uphold me,
    The wisdom of God to teach me,
    The eye of God to watch over me,
    The ear of God to hear me,
    The word of God to give me speech,
    The hand of God to protect me,
    The way of God to go before me,
    The shield of God to shelter me,
    The host of God to defend me,
        Against the snares of demons,
        Against the temptation of vices,
        Against the lusts of nature,
        Against every man who meditates injury to me,
        Whether far or near,
        With few or with many.

He enumerates further dangers to the soul and body, against which he invokes defence, and then breaks into lines that reveal the mystic's union with his Lord—

Christ with me, Christ before me,
Christ behind me, Christ within me,
Christ beneath me, Christ above me,
Christ at my right, Christ at my left,
Christ in the fort,

Christ in the chariot-seat,
Christ in the poop deck:
Christ in the heart of every man who thinks of me,
Christ in the mouth of every man who speaks to me,
Christ in every eye that sees me,
Christ in every ear that hears me—

and he repeats his first verse, invoking the Blessed Trinity.

So singing, the little band came into danger and passed through it. Somewhere in that rich farmland of Meath, the road was beset by rugged, grim men, weapons in hand; they rose from the wayside to do the murderous bidding of the High-King's people. Arms are raised, the spearpoint lifted from the grass; but that strange man from the Roman land, with the harmless staff of crooked handle, does not halt, nor yet those gentle folk who are with him, not even the little *giolla* at the rear with the satchel of writing tablets.

On they go, the fearless nine, chanting their strange Gaelic words: "*Crist lim, Crist rium, Crist im degaid, Crist innium,* Christ with me, Christ before me…Christ in the heart of all who think of me, in every eye that sees me." Strange words, to a solemn, strange chanting air, stirring something in the heart of the hearers never felt before! The spears are lowered. A Fenian warrior, a soldier who has fought with soldiers, cannot strike such men as these; and so the little band goes by, unhurt.

The last lines of the "Breastplate" are in Latin:

Domini est salus,
Domini est salus,
Christi est salus,
Salus tua, Domine, sit semper nobiscum.

"Salvation is of the Lord, salvation is of Christ; may thy salvation, Lord, be forever with us." The holy words of victory melt in the sunlit Irish Easter air.

Tradition says that the ambushers saw naught but eight deer and a fawn upon the road, as if the chant were magical; that is why the piece is called "The Deer's Cry." We can read a very simple explanation into this tradition; for Patrick was no magician.

"Why did you not strike down the Roman stranger, who has come to conquer Ireland?" the plotters would ask the fighting men.

Conceive the answer: "We saw no enemies, but as it were eight deer that went past us, and a fawn with a bundle on the shoulder."

"These were our enemies."

"Sirs, they were gentle as deer."

2. IN THE BANQUETING HALL

The hill of Tara lies in the most fertile part of Leinster, some twenty odd miles from Dublin, a little beyond Duns-haughlin. There, where rising country begins to open on a spacious view away to the Ulster Mountains, a lane to the left climbs a slope which once the chariots of kings ascended. Climb half a mile, and you suddenly find big meadows which are marked by huge green earthworks; the bases of the timber palaces that were here in antiquity. Some of these ramparts are circular, and bear such names as *Ráth Laoghaire* and the Rath of the Synods; and there is one rectangle, seven hundred and fifty-nine feet long by forty-six feet wide, which is known as *Teach Míodhchuarta*, the House of the Circulating Mead, or Banqueting Hall. Grazing cattle wander in and out of the fourteen gaps in the sides of that hall's foundations. Of old, huge poles were rooted in these ramparts, upholding the painted timber walls, and the hill now crowned with these empty green foundations was a brilliant city of timber, a landmark that could be seen afar; for Tara, though not high, looks out over a vast parapet of the Leinster plain, to far-off blue hills and, in winter, snow-capped ranges.

This was the capital of all Ireland in the days of Laoghaire and his father Niall, and had been seat of a High-King at least since the days of Cormac mac Airt, in the third century. Before Cormac, the monarchy of all Ireland is not acknowledged by modern historians, although tradition and the poets told that Tara had been a national capital always, away back to a thousand years before Christ. At any rate there were Kings of Leinster, if not of Ireland, on Tara hill in remote ages. There were sacred Kings there before Homer sang of the Achaeans. The chief Irish archaeologist, Dr. R. A. Stewart Macalister,[2] has dug far beneath the earthen ramparts which remain today from Laoghaire's time, and has traced foundations, cut in the stark rock, which tell of immemorial habitation there, and of the royal hill as a place of pagan sanctity. When Laoghaire was High-King there, Tara as a royal seat of some kind was fully fifteen hundred years old. Long ago as Patrick's coming to Tara is from us, just so long Tara had been a seat of kings when Laoghaire sat there awaiting him.

The High-King, as we read, used to sit at the northern end of the great banquet hall—that hall so long that a voice needed to be raised high to reach from end to end of it. Applying the authentic description of one of Laoghaire's predecessors, we may tell how the king's long curls flowed about his golden collar. He wore a red buckler with golden stars and animals and silver fastenings. His

---

2.   R. A. Stewart Macalister, *Tara: A Pagan Sanctuary of Ancient Ireland.*

cloak was of crimson, clasped with a great jewelled brooch. His linen was embroidered in red-gold thread, and his fine leather shoes were stitched in gold. Such was a High-King of those days.

Beside Laoghaire, at his right hand, sat the queen in splendid satins. To his left were his harpers; behind him his jugglers and clowns. Beyond the queen sat the chief brehon and others. Beyond the harpers sat Druids, poets, and historians. Hostages—young princes from the subordinate, or provincial, kingdoms—were to the right beyond the brehons, and then the long, long tables were lined with the great gentlemen of Meath and their ladies. On the other side were the places for the High-King's guests; ambassadors, and, at the end, the Steward of Tara.

That indicates how a High-King's tables were used. Guards stood at all doors. Shields were on the walls, above their owners' places, and bearing, perhaps, designs like the heraldry of later days. A chain hung from the vaulted roof of that vast timber hall, near the king.

There was an air of doubt, of tension, in that royal place. News had gone through the raths and forts and booths and grassy meeting places of the royal city that the envoy from the Roman world was coming to the king. So those strange pagan folk talked and wondered as they waited. At the booths there would be Greek merchants who were questioned eagerly about that strange thing in the Roman world which a spiritual High-King ruled, sending envoys about the earth who carried no arms. What did it all mean?

In the background of the pressing Irish throng there would be foreign slaves who listened to the gossip with glowing hearts; their eyes burned to gaze on the Bishop of their own faith who was coming, coming, coming to command these pagans, their masters. Within the great banqueting hall, the harpers played to the great folk, who hardly listened to the music, so far away were their minds, wondering, wondering. In the distance, there was the sound of the voice of a throng; something was happening; the crowd about the gates of Tara was crying out.

With a loud jangle, the herald at the king's side shook the chain of silence. The harps and the voices within the royal hall ceased; the noise on the hill swelled loud.

Be sure that the white-robed Druids listened most sharply of all. The guards stood stiff beside their spears, yet almost quivered. The groan of gates was heard and an uproar, that faded and fell in a hush of wonder; and then, with the fulness of liturgic song, nine strong voices chanting the Roman words:

> *Domini est salus,*
> *Domini est salus,*
> *Christi est salus,*
> *Salus tua, Domine, sit semper nobiscum.*

"The gates flew open," says the old account.

Even as the last word was chanted, the doorkeeper stood aside and the High-King saw a prodigy in the doorway at the far end, the south end, of the hall before him—the Cross borne like Roman eagles, entering the royal place of Ireland, where the eagles never came. Perhaps candles were borne, and the flame of them bent in the troubled air.

Still chanting, the company of nine—Britons, Gauls, and convert Irish, with the figure of Patricius marked out by his Roman garb and uplifted head, commanding gaze—moved past the astonished guards and up the long aisle of the hall. Never an envoy from Alba or Pictland or far-off Lochlann of the blue streams had come thus fearlessly to the very seat of the High-King, doors opening before him through sheer, involuntary homage of guards and keepers.

The Bishop passed the steward of Tara, the half-empty places of the envoys and of guests, and came to where the poets and scholars sat: and behold you—two rose to their feet, while all the rest of the great folk of Ireland remained seated, fearing to anticipate the king.

Two rose: Dubthach mac Lugair, chief of the poets of the Gael, and a youth named Fiacc, a student of poetry. These two stood, with hearts afire and heads bent in reverence, as Patricius passed them and signed the cross with his uplifted hand towards them— and who knows but the Christian slaves among the serving folk fell to their knees to catch their share of blessing?

On past the silent and staring harpers and the gaping jugglers, the cross-bearer and the others with Patricius trod, and now the Bishop faced the king.

"I have come, O High-King!"

3. Defeat for Druidry

Still not rising, the scarlet-robed Laoghaire bowed his crowned head a little and said: "You are welcome." He directed the Bishop to be seated beside them, there at the head of the tables. Amazement went through the company of great folk. The stranger from the Roman land had not been sent to the seats far down the hall among the envoys, but had been given the seat of honour, never before offered to a guest!

One there was whose spirit was curdled with hatred at that sight. He was a Druid, one of those teachers of the people who knew that this stranger challenged their command of the minds of men.

This dark soul so hated the Roman missionary that he resolved to slay him. So, as food and drink were served to the weary Bishop, the Druid slipped poison into the cup. Patricius, ever watchful, was not deceived. He blessed the cup before he drank the mead; and the old narrative says that the poison separated from the drink and he cast it forth.

The High-King talked with the Bishop, surprised to find that he talked Irish as if it were his native tongue.

"I was taken slave in my childhood," the prelate would tell. "Your father Niall of the Hostages brought me captive to Ireland: but God willed it so."

What strange man was this, high of rank in that strange spiritual kingdom oversea, who was not ashamed to speak of his slavery and his herding of swine; but rather gloried in it?

"I used to sleep out on the rough side of Slemish mountain," the Bishop said, half speaking to himself and smiling softly, as men do when they remember their distant youth. "In frost and rain and storm, I loved to be alone on the Irish mountainside; for so I was near to God."

Strange hearing was this for the High-King in his scarlet robe and golden splendour!

There came to the king, when Patricius was refreshed, a Druid who asked him to bring the stranger to the green gathering place on Tara, till he would show him the power of the Druids. Patricius assented, when Laoghaire asked if this was agreeable; so king and Bishop, followed by the notables of Tara, went forth to the April fields, under blue Spring sky. The wondering folk of the royal city gathered to look on at what would follow.

"Let us bring snow upon this great plain," the Druid's spokesman said.

"I wish to bring nothing that is contrary to God's will," said the Bishop.

A smile of triumph went through the pagan circle; and the incantations began. Laoghaire saw that smile and turned his eyes upon the woodland and bogland and meadow and ploughed field of the western plain—and saw a great fall of snow suddenly gather upon it. Thick, thick and white was that druidic snow, drowning the Springtime scene.

That was an ancient, much-favoured illusion of the Druids, some strange hypnotic feat. Their power was not lessened yet. King and people were deceived by that strange spell.

Patricius, however, seemed nothing daunted. "You have brought this thing, now take it away!" he said.

Trembling and pale through his great effort of the will, the Druid shook his head. "I cannot take it away till tomorrow," he answered.

"You are strong for evil, weak for good," said the Bishop; "and now," he cried, speaking with the ringing voice of authority, "behold the power of the God who is Three in One!"

To south and west and north, he blessed the Irish plain with the sign of the cross; and that phantom snowfall vanished and the sunlit land was seen!

Then it was, perhaps, that the wondering and uplifted listeners cried out to Patricius the Bishop to tell them more of this strange God, whose nature he had described with the Triune Name; and that he, after plucking shamrock from the field at his feet, spoke to them of the Trinity with the little green leaf as its emblem.

Tradition says, although there are no documents to confirm the popular belief, that he so used the shamrock. Certain it is, from his own writings, that the Triune nature of God was foremost in his teaching. Across Europe, the heresy of Arianism, which denied the Trinity, had spread in those days, and was held by the barbarian peoples. Patricius, therefore, taught the doctrine of the Trinity at the very outset, to make clear that he was no Arian, and that he came with the voice of unchanging Rome.

So favourable was the Bishop's reception by king and people that he asked and gained permission, then and there, to go forward in his lifelong purpose: to preach and to organise the Church throughout Ireland.

"I believe that what you teach is right," Laoghaire probably said. "I would have my nation to accept your Roman faith and not that of the Arians, who are between us and Rome."

Yet the High-King would not be baptised. His word was enough to cause numbers of those lords and gentry and common folk, of Tara to seek baptism; but he stood apart, *laudator temporis acti.*

"For me," he may have said, "I am bound by my father's wishes. Great Niall bade me to hold fast to the ways of the kings of Tara, and to be buried in the walls of the city with my weapons and my face to the foe. Go you on with your work, and may you prosper; but I will stand by the old ways."

That is what happened; but St. Patrick went forth on the task before him, in the cause of his own King.

CHAPTER VII

The Fall of an Idol

1. DONAGHPATRICK

From Tara, five military roads, that had been made in the third century in imitation of the Roman roads and as a measure for the defence of Ireland against invasion from the Roman road, radiated to the Irish provinces. That which led to the north-west lay beside the lazy Blackwater, through Ceanannus Mór (of Kells), and by Lough Ramor's pleasant, reedy shore.

On the north bank of the river, ten miles from Tara, a strong place of triple ramparts stood. This was given to Patricius the Bishop, when the High-King granted him leave to organise the Christian Church in Ireland, at Easter in the year 433. The Bishop built a church there and set up his missionary headquarters, for the first stage of his work. It is called Donaghpatrick to this day. When Donagh appears in a place-name, it usually means that Patrick founded a church there.

The Bishop had his scribes copying Missals, his metalworkers making chalices, his charioteers preparing transport, within the triple rath there in rich Meath.

Two years passed thus in hard but congenial work, while the Bishop meditated his second great challenge to paganism. Forty miles distant, in a fastness of misty mountain, moorland, boulder-sprinkled plain, bog, and tangled boughs, there stood a strange, heathen shrine. At the end of summer, pilgrimages went thither, the High-King himself riding with the people, to practise rites of darkness and of terror. That shrine must be laid low.

Patricius questioned folk who had made that pilgrimage. They answered in a voice of awe.

"Cromm Cruach, Cromm Cruach," they would answer, naming the god of wrath whom they had worshipped.

"He is dangerous to offend," some frank-faced Meath-man would say, and the honest eyes would be clouded with fear. "Our High-King Cormac defied him, and the curse of Cromm Cruach struck him dead."

Others would recall King Tighernmas of the very ancient times, the King of all Ireland who was the first smelter of gold, and how the dread god of Magh Sleacht had blasted him and all his people, for some offence.

The two poets who had been the Bishop's converts when he entered the hall of Tara may have told him more about the god of the misty plain.

"This Cromm Cruach," Mac Lugair would say, "is a monster of stone, gilded and strange to behold. It stands at Magh Sleacht, in a circle of smaller bronze-clad stones, and our people have worshipped there from ages beyond even the memory of the poets. It is in the name of Cromm that our people are haunted by *geasa*, or prohibitions. They may not do this or that, without dread of ill luck. Our wiser Druids know that this is folly, but they cannot reason the people out of their dread.

"No man will start an undertaking on a Friday, no king will ride forth from Leinster on a Monday. Say that it is foolish to believe in Cromm's power, and they will answer: 'Ah, but if it should be true!'"

Patricius had met this dark obstacle in men's minds. The people of Ireland were burdened with innumerable *geasa*—strange, unreasoning prohibitions. Every calamity that befell them, they ascribed to the offended god. Blight on a crop, an accident on the road, a child's death—every sorrow was to them a blow from malicious powers, powers that they tried to pacify with sacrifice. Men who had suffered a run of misfortune would take their youngest children to Magh Sleacht and slay them before the gilded stone.

Such was the superstition which the Firbolg, or some dark breed before them, had fastened on men's souls, and never had any risen with courage to shake it off.

"Christ shall prevail," Patricius said to Mac Lugair and Fiacc, the poets, and to Conall, the King's brother: "and Cromm Cruach must be cast down before the eyes of all. I will do it with these hands."

The converts saw the light of high resolve upon the Bishop's countenance; they crushed down the misgivings of their hearts and rose.

"We will go with you," they said to this strange, fearless cleric.

2. The Plain of Adoration

When the meadows of July were like a green sea rippled by wind-driven waves, Patricius the Bishop and his clerics and first converts travelled forth from Meath.

Immediately north of Ceanannus Mór, the rich land changes to gravelly hills and heath; it is airy, lovely country, but wild. Just where the road to Magh Sleacht lay, we cannot be sure. A book says that the company went by Granard and Cloone or Mohill—but, whether or not, it led at last to what now we call Garadise Lough, and there the little caraven must halt.

Chariot and wagon and horses must go no farther than the reedy shore of those shallow waters, beyond which the travellers saw rising land with the vast, cloud-wrapped Slieve-an-Iarainn against the distant sky. The Mountain of Iron! Patricius gazed on it, no doubt, as all do when they see it first, wondering, so bleak, so bare it is, and mysterious. It is easy to understand why the story-tellers say that the magical invaders of Ireland in the dawn of time landed from a cloud on Slieve-an-Iarainn.

In the days of Patricius, there was something stranger even than this to arrest the eye—Cromm Cruach!

Beyond the lake, on a little limestone hill in Magh Sleacht, the Plain of Adoration, reflected in the water as if the land floated between two worlds, stood the great idol, gleaming in gold through the summer haze, with the the bronze-clad minor idols in a ramparted circle around it. It was an uncouth monster, vaguely human-seeming in shape. On many hills in Ireland to this day the *Fir Bréaga*, the Mock-Men, groups of leaning stones, still give the same strange appearance of unearthly giants.

Within the charmed circle, men could be seen moving in ritual mode. A sound of wailing or of wild, staccato chants, floated on the summer air.

No doubt, the fears which hung about the place touched the spirits of some who were with the Bishop, but his high-held features gave the doubters courage, and we can picture what followed.

As the Bishop went aboard the boat, made of a hollowed tree-trunk, in which pilgrims crossed the narrow lough, rowed by sweeps that three bare-bodied giants pulled, Patricius signalled to his deacons, and mark you, in place of the loud cries from which the lake was named *Guthárd,* or "Loud Voice," now called Garadice, there rose the measured Latin chant:

> *Quare fremuerunt Gentes, et populi*
> *meditati sunt inania…*
> *Dirumpamus vincula eorum…*

The rowers were amazed as this firm-faced stranger in the Roman garb stood and faced the Idol of Fear, and chanted the unknown words: "Why have the Gentiles raged, and the people devised vain things? … Let us break their bonds asunder: and let us cast away their yoke from us.… "

The words swelled as the Bishop's courage lifted the hearts of his people, and David's psalm became a song of battle.

An old, dark-minded stock, the Masraighe, then inhabited that place and tended the monstrous gods of stone and metal. They stared through their glibs at the clerics and the convert scholars, who landed on the north bank and began to walk in processional order, led by the Cross, the *Vexillum* of the new faith, up the half-mile of road towards the sacred acre. Hatred was in the eyes that watched, evil wishes were spoken by the muttering tongues. Yet none dared oppose these unarmed strangers; for with them walked Conall, brother of the High-King, in his cloak hemmed with the Seven Colours of Nobility. Conall was the guide and the guard of the Roman. Not once did the procession halt. On went the Cross and the following clerics, and Benignus carrying the holy books and Patricius last in the ceremonial cloak which we would call a chasuble. They made no obeisance. They never looked on the officers of the god who sought to stay them. Straight through the gap on the circular rampart, past the bronze minor-gods, they went, until they reached the gilded monster and the clerics stood to right and left, and Patricius advanced to the centre and faced at last Cromm Cruach, the god of fear and blood.

3. CHALLENGE TO CROMM

Magh Sleacht lies in the diocese of Kilmore, the historian whereof[1] has reconstructed the mysterious business of Patrick's challenge to Cromm Cruach, in a manner which we follow, as we try to visualise the event. The Plain of Adoration lies under and before Slieve-an-Iarainn, the Mountain of Iron, where the high, rolling thunder must have seemed to the people of ancient days the very voice of their god, so that Cromm got as his name a word which imitates the thunder's muttering. On Magh Sleacht, within an ancient rampart, a church stands today where Patrick founded one, after his victory: the church of Kilnavart.

Some say that the High-King himself, Laoghaire, the son of Niall, was at Magh Sleacht when the Christian company approached. It was the eve of August, when, in the hush of the year, the old race used to worship the fearsome powers of Nature, hoping for a favourable harvest. It was usual for the High-King to be among those who prostrated themselves before the gilded pillar-stone, in the circle of the Fir Bréaga.

---

1. Philip O'Connell, *The Diocese of Kilmore*. Dr. O'Connell makes a strong case, from local tradition, for the historicity of St. Patrick's destruction of Cromm Cruach, and we have used his work chiefly in our attempt to reconstruct and visualise the event. In an essay *On the Medieval Sources for the Legend of Cenn (Crom) Croich of Magh Slecht* (1940), Mr. Michael O Duigeannain, M.A., of the National Museum, Dublin, investigates the documentary evidence and arrives at an open conclusion.

Yet, as we have seen, Laoghaire had given Patricius leave to Christianise the Kingdom of Ireland, and he himself chose to remain a pagan—to live and to die like the lords of Ireland before him. After him, new times would bring new ways, He knew it, and forbade it not.

Surely, then, when the strange man of the books and the bells who came to organise the new order went forth to challenge Cromm Cruach in his shrine, Laoghaire neither aided nor interfered. He remained at Tara, and let the new order take its course. Instead of a High-King, embodying his nation's obedience to the pagan ways, there had come to Magh Sleacht this company of Christians, chanting psalms instead of hushing their voices, and marching boldly to the very idol's base instead of bowing to the earth.

Why did the custodians of the shrine make no resistance when the Bishop gave orders and his servants began, with spades and crowbars, to attack the very foundation of the idol? Perhaps, the very absence of the High-King was a signal that the Roman cleric's act had his approval. Perhaps, the very audacity of this unarmed company's challenge to the Thunderer (and now no thunder rolled from the heights above, on that blue July day) overcame the would-be defenders of Cromm.

Most likely of all, Conall, the Christian brother of the High-King, overawed the guardians of the shrine, though he never unsheathed the shapely sword that he carried; he and his few followers stood when the High-King would have kneeled, and watched what was done, with faces drawn and pale.

The eager hands that piled the fires of Slane two years before now made short work of the undermining of the idol. A lever was worked upon the fulcrum of a log, and the great, gold-clad monster tilted.

"Ah!"—a gasp went up from the furtive gazers-on, who were drawn towards the green rampart by curiosity that was stronger than fear.

Patricius gave a signal. The bare-armed toilers stood back. Benignus drew back a fold of the chasuble from the arm of the Bishop, who lifted the *Bachall Iosa*, the sacred staff, strengthened with metal, that he always carried. Now, with the casing of metal that one of his craftsmen had made by Patrick's command, it was raised like a sword—a new Sword of Light wielded under the Irish sun.

Patricius lifted *Bachall Iosa*, crying, perhaps, in a loud voice: "*In nomine Dei*"—and thrust. His blow struck the gilded toppling idol, and down the monster fell with a thudding blow that shook the earth and sent dust flying high. A shriek of fear went up, and then there was a hush as folk waited for the darkening of the sky and the thunder that never came.

Cromm Cruach was overthrown!

The old accounts treat this deed of Patrick's as a miracle, so greatly did it loom in the memory of men. Yet the event was plain enough, and its lesson was simple. Patricius and his people had defied the Thunderer. They had not knelt while he stood; but now, when the place of him was bare, they did kneel. They knelt to pray now, not to Cromm.

The clasp of the Bishop's chasuble was lost in his exertion. Somewhere in the heather before the empty site of the idol it lay. He caused the heather to be cut away as the clasp was sought. This little homely detail is remembered after 1500 years.

Within a double rath, there stood the house of the keeper of the shrine. This was given to Patricius, and he dedicated it as a church. A priest named Methbrain was left in charge of this station among the Masraighe, as the unfriendly folk of that place were named.

Three holy wells there still commemorate the work of Patricius. From them, no doubt, he drew the water which he blessed as he sanctified the pagan shrine.

4. THE VENGEANCE

The years passed in golden summers and grey winters, and under Slieve-an-Iarainn a Christian community grew. Yet there were folk within whose hearts the anger of Cromm still smouldered, the dark-minded Masraighe who never forgave the strange cleric from oversea, the breaker of their olden ways. Most of all, Conall of Meath, of the free-born brow and noble soul, was hated—the protector of the cleric.

A tradition describes something that happened, when, after thirty years, news came from afar off that Patricius was dead. With sorrowing chant, no doubt, Mass was celebrated for him a Kilnavart, where Cromm Cruach was only a memory among the middle-aged and the old.

A little later, the story says, Conall of Meath came to that country. He, the royal and noble, grey-bearded, yet upright still, stood there, remembering the distant day when Patricius had overthrown the god of fear and wrath. There was a grave joy in that kingly heart as Conal remembered that he had been privileged to take part in aid of the work of Patricius, now in heaven, having spread the peace of Christ in the place of the wrath of Cromm. Even as he breathed a thankful prayer, Conall staggered. A spear had been driven through his back. Cromm Cruach's people, now that Patricius was dead, had avenged their idol. Conall fell to earth, slain by the Masraighe with a coward's blow—but his soul followed that of Patrick.

CHAPTER VIII

The Faith Wins Connacht

1. THE SHANNON CROSSED

When Patrick had established the Church in Meath, and had destroyed Cromm Cruach, he carried his sacred campaign into the West. Kilmore diocese, which comprises the counties of Leitrim and Cavan, was reckoned part of Connacht then; for Cavan was not included in Ulster's boundary until the sixteenth century. At Magh Sleacht, Patrick already stood in Connacht; but he had not crossed the Shannon. He must have been anxious to conquer the West—to plant his churches and bishoprics, and to found mission stations throughout that strange, strange region—and so to bring the faith even to the ocean's edge, *ubi nemo ultra erat*, to use his own phrase, "beyond which no man dwelt." If he succeeded in the West, as he had in the Royal province of Meath, he would carry the frontier of Christendom out to the end of the known earth, far, far beyond the frontier of the declining Roman Empire, which ended with the coast of Britain.

Such, surely was the feeling, the ambition which fired him as he commanded his mission caravan, his covered wagons with altar-stones, crosses, books, vestments, his clerics and craftsmen and serving-folk, to take the road which led to the fords of the Shannon.

The mysterious, misty heights of Slieve-an-Iarainn gloomed in
the sky to the right hand, and the road wound in and out through
the bog and marsh of the watery, undrained countryside, with many
a wild-bird-haunted, sedgy lake, and of human settlements on hills
that rose from the moisture. To this day, the market towns of Kilmore are perched on little hills, like folk who stand on mounds in
a flood. It would be where the land improves into broad, sloping
pastures round Carrick on Shannon that the river was reached. The
destination of the caravan was Rathcroghan, in the centre of our
county Roscommon, the kingly stronghold of Connacht, ancient
and like Tara sacred to the pagan mind.

Cruachain!—ramparted with dry-stone walls, an immemorial
fortress: this was where the fabled Queen Meave, in the century
before Christ died, had planned great conquests and had mustered
innumerable hosts of fighting men, with chariots and leather tents
and bronze spears and the new, short, iron swords. "Cruachain!"—
the name was battle-cry that had been shouted across all Ireland
once, and had gone up hoarsely from the western queen's plunder-
ing legions as they battled a way to the far-off coast of the north
that looks to the unreached isles of Alba. For a thousand years
before Patricius, the old, old western race had feasted and clashed
its weapons here; and for a thousand years yet to come there would
be kings and princes and proud gentry of the name of O Connor,
who would boast of Cruachain as their royal city, though it sank
to stony desolation, and lived like Troy, only as a city of the soul.

The High-Kings of Ireland were a Connacht family, that had
thrust from Cruachain eastward across the Shannon, and northward from Tara into Ulster. They still had Cruachain as a royal seat.
The High-King Niall's nephew, Daithi, had succeeded him in 405
and had reigned until he died abroad, on a raiding expedition, in

428, and Niall's son Laoghaire had succeeded. Daithi was buried at Cruachain, and a vast red sandstone pillar which still is standing was erected over his grave. That pillar-stone was about ten years standing when Patrick came to Cruachain.

Perhaps it was at evening, weary after the fifteen miles' journey from the Shannon fords, that the priestly expedition came in sight of the high ramparts and ancient cairns, which the labour of innumerable toilers long ago had piled. At any rate, it is certain that the company camped for the night outside the western fortress; for a tale is told of something that befell at early morning there, in a clearing between rocks where a spring flowed, a spring immortally famous as the Well of Clebach.

2. At Clebach Well

At a place where the limestone outcropped from the shallow soil, and the sweet, fine grass was like a carpet, the encampment was astir before dawn, and those bishops who were with Patricius were walking aside with him to plan the movement of the day, when two royal maidens came by the dusty white western road, making for the clear, cool spring.

They were daughters of Laoghaire, the High-King; for the Royal clan that ruled Ireland from Tara, as we have said, still used its olden home.

Eithne the White and Fedelm the Red, these western maidens were named. They were dwelling at Cruachain, fostered and taught by two Druids, Mael and Caplait. We can but guess how they were attired—the cloaks clasped with brooches of filigree, the golden ornaments that bound the long strands of their hair.

The old writers say that the girls wondered at the strangers—
Patricius and his bishops, in their stately Roman garb, like the vestments that are worn at Mass. They thought, for a moment, that
these majestic figures, seen in the pale mist of the dawn, were folk
of the immortal, magical race of the Tuatha De Danann; which
illusion, perhaps, the Latin speech of the clerics aided.

These schoolgirls never had heard any speech but Irish, never
had seen the dress of the great folk of the Roman world. The fables
of the Tuatha De Danann were less strange to them than the
appearance of clerics from Gaul. They spoke to Patricius, embold-
ened by his gentle bearing:

"Whence have you come?—where is your dwelling?"

Were the strangers from another world? Were their homes in
the mystic dwellings of the immortals, under the mountains and
beyond the palpable earth?

Patrick gently answered: "It would be better for you to believe
in the true God whom we worship than to ask questions about our
race."

Patrick spoke in their own tongue to the maidens—in the Irish
that he had learnt as a slave-boy in Antrim thirty years earlier.

In that homely speech, he said in effect: "We are no supernatural beings, we are men, and it is our message that matters. We
preach God Himself."

This story is told in two of the most ancient lives of the saint;
it stands out from the many doubtful fables about him, and surely
is true.

Let us give, then, what the elder girl said, as the Bishop spoke of
fior-Dhia, the True God. The girlish inquiries have come down the
centuries as fresh and curious and simple as when Eithne uttered
them, probably in the year 434:

Who is God? Where is God? Of whom is God? Where is His dwelling? Has he sons and daughters, this God of yours, and has he gold and silver? Is He ever living? Is He fair?

To these questions, Patrick made answer—sitting on the chair of limestone that Nature had provided, no doubt, while the quick-eyed girls listened eagerly. He spoke of God omnipotent, *Pater et Filius, et Spiritus Sanctus*; for the next questions, as the old books tell, were:

Has His Son been fostered by many? Are His daughters fair to the men of the world and fair in their eyes?

To these questions in turn we can guess Patrick's answer. He tried to make these little pagan lassies understand the nature of divinity. This we can see by the next questions, as the old books record them:

Is He in heaven or in earth?—in the sea, in the rivers, in the hill places, in the valleys? Tell us how we may know Him, in what manner He will appear. How is He discovered? Is He found in youth or in old age?

That last question shows the girl who asked it deeply moved. Must a child, she wondered, wait till old age to be holy like this grey-haired teacher?

The answer is one of the utterances of Patrick which reveal at once the splendour of his mind and his peculiar aptitude for the work that he undertook. He had come to a land of Druids who were half poet and of poets who were half Druid; where the Sun was worshipped, and the supernatural was identified with Nature's wonders. How fitly he answered the question of the girls at Clebach Well, girls who had a Druid education! He said:

Our God is the God of all men, the God of heaven and earth, of sea and rivers, of sun and moon and stars, of the lofty mountain and the lowly valleys, the God above heaven and in heaven, and under heaven; He has His dwelling around heaven and earth and sea and all that in them is.

He inspires all, He quickens all, He dominates all, He supports all.

He lights the light of the sun, He furnishes the light of the night; He has made springs in the dry land, and has set stars to minister to the greater lights.

He has a Son co-eternal with Himself, and like unto Himself. The Son is not younger than the Father, nor the Father older than the Son; and the Holy Spirit breathes in Them. The Father, the Son and the Holy Spirit are not divided.

I wish to unite you with the heavenly King, as ye are daughters of an earthly king. Believe!

The story then tells that the High-King's daughters, with one heart and one voice, declared their desire to accept Patrick's God. They went under instruction, and were catechised briefly.[1]

"Do you believe that by baptism original sin is taken away?"

---

1.   Archbishop Healy, *Life and Writings of St. Patrick.*

"We believe it."

"Do you believe in penance as a remedy for sin?"

"We believe it."

"Do you believe in the unity of the Church?"

"We believe it."

Having required of the maidens their assent to the Apostles' Creed, the Bishop baptised them in that wellspring where they had met him. They had come to refresh the body, but they remained to receive immortal life. A white veil was put on each young head. Instantly, as the ancient account tells, these new-baptised souls were seized with desire for Heaven, for the vision of God. Strangely the story continues, with a sense of wonder that comes down fifteen centuries, to tell how the maidens received the Blessed Eucharist forthwith, and fell asleep; they died—died of sheer desire for the beatific vision.

The rugged old pagan at Tara, who permitted the teaching of the faith that he would not accept, evidently had given his daughters a determined nature. Such were two of Ireland's first nuns, and first mystics; and this, as it is one of the best authenticated things written of our Apostle, so it also is one of those which we can recognise instantly as true to character, both of the Apostle and of the womanhood of Ireland.

3. Croagh Patrick

The labours of Patrick in Meath, part of Ulster, and Connacht occupied seven years. He made three journeys into the West. "Fifty bells and fifty chalices and fifty altar-cloths he left in Connacht, each in its own church."

Sees in Connacht recall with poetic names the Apostle's labours. Today, it is strangely moving to see a road-side sign-post point to Ardagh—*Ard-achadh*, the High Field—where he installed St. Mel, a holy Briton, as bishop, or a motor-coach go by at night with a lighted panel that announces its destination in Elphin—*Ail-Fionn*, the White Cliff—where the Apostle's copper-smith, St. Assicus, was first bishop. One of the churches which Patrick founded is marked today by the name of a village, Baislec, near Rathcroghan. That name is the modern rendering of the proud original name, *Basilica Sanctorum*; for the church established there was of particular importance, a basilica enriched with relics of the Apostles Peter and Paul and the martyrs Stephen and Laurence[2] which it shared with the primatial see of Armagh. It would occupy a pious pilgrim long to visit all the spots in Connacht where holy wells and teeming traditions commemorate the labours of the saint in that triumphant western campaign. When at length he had planted the faith securely from the Shannon to the western ocean; had set up bishoprics and churches, had won kings and Druids to the faith, queenly maidens to the convent: when, in a word, he knew that great Connacht of the amethystine walls and misty mountains and splendid forests (for there were woods in plenty, then, of primeval fir and oak and elm; but the beech had not come yet)—then, at Lent in the year 440, Patrick made a solitary retreat on the summit of Cruachan Aigle the Reek, which we also call Croagh Patrick.

The journey to the Reek he made by chariot. We read that his charioteer, Totmael (the Wholly Bald One), died at the foot of the mountain, and that the Bishop buried him there and heaped stones around the tomb: the stones are there still, easily identified.

---

2.   Eoin MacNeill, *Saint Patrick*.

"May it remain so forever; and it shall be visited by me in the last days," said the Bishop, ere he turned to climb the mountain.

This western height, shaped like a long wave before it breaks, is an enormous grey landmark, visible from half Connacht and from far at sea. It is near the ocean's edge, where Ireland ends in a craggy bay and multitudes of little islands. It is bare and harsh, sprinkled with rocks and boulders and splinters of stone, gouged with the channels of torrents, beaten upon by the oceanic clouds, bleak, stark, terrible and yet splendid. Every July, on the last Sunday, tens of thousands of pilgrims climb from the shore road up the pathless slopes, and Masses are said by many priests on the sublime summit, before the kneeling multitude. To see the pilgrimage to Croagh Patrick, traditional among the western people since ancient days, is to see the old race and its very soul. Here you are knit to the innermost thoughts of unforgetting Gaeldom.

What a place in which to endure, as Patrick did, the rigours of a western March and early April, when black clouds lie around and below that summit, changing into torrential rain that thunders through the precipitous water channels, and rocks tumble with the cataracts! Which of the strongest of us could endure such a penance? Even in bright July, when the sun beats through the purest air of Europe, to climb that rough mountainside, from height to higher height, is bitterly hard. Hear the account of a stalwart farmer from Kildare.[3]

> Onwards and upwards we go. The track becomes rougher and consists of stones embedded in greasy mud. A Cork man in a shining oilskin turns round to

---

3. Stephen Rynne, *Green Fields.*

me: "Have you ever been up before?" he lilts, Cork-
wise. I answer "No." "Do you think we have gone up
much of it?" he continues. I tell him I imagine we have
made a good start. "Well, I don't think it's as bad as I
thought it would be," he says, and on he goes, delighted
with my encouragement, swaying his glistening pos-
terior before me. Poor babies that we were! We knew
nothing.

I overtake two girls, sixteen or seventeen, lissome,
and climbing like deers; one was giving out the Rosary,
and the other answering it.

The rain eased off for a time. "Oh, St. Patrick, St. Patrick, St. Patrick," wailed a woman behind, "what made
you go up so high at all?" I passed out old men and poor
stout women struggling valiantly along. A young girl going barefoot passed me out. At no time could one see
far ahead, which limitation was a great mercy. When we
had about a mile accomplished of the three and a half in
the ascent, we began to see people coming down. Soon
there were as many people coming down as going up.
The mountainside paths were thronged.

Up and up we toiled through the mist and drizzle,
keeping to the meerest token of a pathway, over rocks
and stones, through ooze and mire, quaking bogs and
landslides. Then a time came when we reached a level
zone and my worn heart took courage; actually the track
seemed to lead downwards. Oh, St. Patrick, are we really going downhill, or is it only a sweet illusion? More
proximate than St. Patrick was a kindly looking man in
a raincoat; after the proper preamble I put my pressing

question to him: "Are we nearly up?" My man is astonished and looks at me quickly. "Oh no, we don't start the
climb until we get to the first station." Feel for my feel-
ings! Very soon, however, we reach the point called by
some the first station (though I prefer to think the be-
nign statue which now seems miles below us, and as remote as a childhood prank, is the real first station). This
second "first station," then, is a bed of stones marking
the place where St. Patrick's companion was killed when
he went ahead of his master to investigate conditions
on the mountain-top. We walk around this station the
regulation number of times and recite a given number
of prayers, imploring at the end of each round that St.
Patrick would shield Ireland from present enemies as he
had vouchsafed to shield her in the past.

So Stephen Rynne begins. He continues thus:

Then we start climbing the Reek in earnest, and truly
all that we had hitherto done seemed a lover's amble in
comparison. I, who am hardy, young, and active, felt
like thistledown in a cement-mixer when confronted
with this terrible Reek. What a purgatory of a climb!
Every stone is a rock on Croagh Patrick, and a whop-
ping big rock! What sharp stones, flinty stones, slip-
pery stones, greasy stones, yielding stones, angular
stones, stones of every size and weight, stony-heart-
ed and brutal stones, worse than flames, or floods, or
plagues of stinging pests. The downcoming pilgrims
tease us, telling us that we haven't far to go, when there

are plainly infernal miles still before us; or assuring us that we have a great distance to go, when we are within sight, yes, but far from being within grasp of the prize.

Sheets of drifting white mist obscure the tormented faces of the climbers; laughter and jests have long since died in us; prayers have dried up, except amongst the very devout; there is no joy, or comfort, or rest, or safety in our miserable lives. We cannot stay where we are, with danger of death at one side and a fierce acclivity on the other. But it is not cold, nor is it hot, nor is one hungry though fasting, nor suffering from thirst. In addition to myself, I am carrying up a sopping wet overcoat. I feel that I am dragging the weight of fifty houses, ships, steam-engines, and thousands of bricks and concrete blocks up a merciless precipice.

I am nearly spent. I take more and more time in resting. I am almost hopeless. Then wigwams appear; tiny shelters from which dark-skinned women glare over minerals and teacups; the smell of turf fires reaches my nostrils. Have we arrived? Surely we have! And I was game for another hundred yards at least!

Oh, God, I cannot explain or make anyone understand. God, who knowst every source, what was the beginning of my transformation? Do all men, do dirty men and ribald men, and self-centred men, undergo transfiguration on mountain-tops? Do new worlds spring out of every peak? Is it that angels are made of mists, that saints are boulders, that the stuff of heaven is really mountain granite such as this? Is Christ veritably a Rock? How else am I to account for my alteration? I was corrupt, and

now my corruption is commuted into a spiritual eleva-
tion. It all came in a flash; I was aware of no transitional
stage. Climbing the Reek, I was flesh; here I am bodiless;
nay, far better, I am a released soul. Croagh Patrick takes
the world out of a man of the world and leaves him rec-
ognising himself as a spirit.

For a moment I stand stock still, this miraculous
novelty of possessing a new soul transfixing me to
the ground. Then I force a passage through the dense
crowds and join the pack of crushing humanity outside
the chapel.

Such is the account of a hardy young modern. The Bishop
Patricius, in his early fifties, made that climb and then stayed forty
days and nights on the wind-swept, rain-lashed, bare, cruel summit, fasting, fasting, and praying. Remember that he had been
reared in Roman Britain in a home with tiled floors and hot baths,
servants and ease. What sent this highly civilised cleric to so wild
and harsh a penance? It was some tremendous motion of the spirit,
some triumphant and terrific passion that called for such excessive
expression.

Aye, and this is what exalted the man who had been reared
(very likely) in Pembroke, where from the last outpost of the Roman
world he could look across the Irish Sea to the purple, mysterious
peaks of Wicklow—namely, the knowledge that he had carried the
frontier of Christendom victoriously to the world's end. That was
Patrick's glory, as he gazed from that height in Connacht out to the
grey wintry waters that foamed about the habitable earth. These
last rocks of the earth were part of Christendom.

4. The Angelic Promises

On Shrove Saturday, the Bishop made the ascent. His purpose was
to fast the forty days of Lent, following the example of Moses, of
Elias, and of our Blessed Lord; so the old record tells, and "above
all to pray for the people of Ireland, and he was resolved to do vio-
lence to heaven until his petitions were granted."

He was tormented by enormous clouds of black birds, like
demons, that beat about him; he rang his bell against them, and at
length flung it at them, so that a piece was broken from it—so the
story goes. An angel came at length to console the weary, worn,
and harassed saint, and to announce God's granting of his prayers.
Patrick was promised that his people should hold the faith, even to
the end of time; that a great sea should overwhelm Ireland seven
years before the Judgment day, so that the race should escape the
last anguish of the world; that the Saxons (at that date invading
his native Britain and subjecting the Celtic-Roman people) never
should hold Ireland by consent or force while he was in heaven;
and "that every one of us doing penance even in his last hour will
not be doomed to hell on the last day."

A final petition Patrick made; "that on the day when the twelve
Thrones shall be on Mount Sion, that is on the day of Doom, I
myself shall be judge over the men of Erin on that day."

"This surely cannot be had from God," said the angel.

Patrick refused to leave the mountain unless it was granted;
and he went to say Mass while the angel returned to heaven with
the strange demand.

At nones, the angel returned. "All heaven's powers have inter-
ceded for thee," he said, "and thy petition is granted. You are the
most excellent man that has appeared since the Apostles, save for

your obduracy; but you have prayed and you have obtained. Strike thy bell now and fall on thy knees, and a blessing will come on thee from heaven. All the men of Erin, living and dead, shall be blessed and consecrated to God through thee."

"A blessing on the bountiful King who has given it all," said Patrick; "and now I leave the Reek."

Such is the legend of Patrick's wrestling with the angel for the men of Ireland, as the old writers told it, developing his prayers for his children into this dramatic tale. What went on between the soul of the saint and God, with whom the mystic lived in such close union, could not be told in words, unless some such fabulous dialogue was invented. It suffices us that no less bold a legend could symbolise the saint's Lent-long prayer of union, for the land and people whom he had linked to heaven.

CHAPTER IX

Those Who Helped

1. ROMAN APPROBATION

Under the year 441, the Irish Annals have this entry: "Leo was ordained Bishop of the Roman Church, and Patrick was confirmed (*probatus est*) in the Catholic faith." In these words, the triumph of the mission to Ireland is signalised.

In the year 440, Pope Sixtus III died. At that time, an eminent Italian prelate was in Gaul as an envoy of the emperor. He was elected to the Holy See and crowned pope in September; the Church knows him as St. Leo I, and history as Leo the Great— the pope who overruled the turbulence of the Council of Ephesus, which he flatly called a Thieves' Kitchen (*latrocinium*), overhauled the administration of Rome and curbed erratic movements in Gaul and Spain, subdued rebellion in Constantinople, and, at the Council of Chalcedon, defined the Church's teaching concerning the union of two natures in the Person of Christ. This great theologian, ruler, and administrator, had held high office when St. Celestine was pope, and therefore must have been familiar with the affair of the Irish mission when it was set afoot nine years before. The annalists were aware, no doubt, of the importance of Leo's pontificate, in the exaltation of the Holy See and the discipline of the Universal Church; but they are concerned with its particular bearing on Ireland. Therefore, as we have seen, they couple the Pope's accession with an event which took place in the following year—the approbation of St. Patrick.

Eight years, the Apostle had laboured in Ireland. He had been astonishingly successful; for the Church now was established and organised in Royal Meath and in Ulster and Connacht, and the rulers of a hitherto pagan nation had been won, if not for the faith themselves, for the country's conversion. From Croagh Patrick, when he made his great Lenten thanksgiving and petition in 440, Patrick had sent an account of his achievement to Rome—so it is affirmed—and the new pontiff considered that report and approved it. *Probatus est*: the approval of the Holy See was Patrick's victory.

It is held by many chief historians, including Bury, that Patrick received the Holy Father's approval in person—that he went to Rome. The second oldest Life of Patrick, that written by Tirechán in the seventh century, says that Patrick went to Rome at this time, accompanied by his disciple Sacellus, a western youth and convert, whom he ordained in the Holy City. What more natural than that the Bishop should make this journey to Rome at this stage in his work? He had carried the faith to the western shores, and at this very moment a churchman in Gaul had become pope, one who had been in touch with the sponsors of the mission, Celestine, Germanus, and Palladius. Well might Patrick hasten *ad limina apostolorum*, to follow or to make his report and to seek favours for his undertaking from the new Pontiff. We may assume safely, therefore, that the Apostle of Ireland went to Rome in 441. His eyes rested on that obelisk which witnessed the martyrdom of St. Peter, and which stands today, removed some little distance from its site in Patrick's day, in the great *piazza*.

The favours that Patrick sought he certainly received at this time. Whether they were sent to him in Ireland, as one account tells, or whether he received them in person from Pope Leo as eminent historians believe, Patrick was granted a remarkable treasury of relics. These were relics of the Apostles Peter and Paul and of the martyrs Stephen and Laurence; and it is said that a sheet with Christ's Blood thereon and hair of our Lady were with them. The number of these relics was over three hundred; they were designed for the newly founded churches, far and wide. The chief of them were enshrined with great honour at Armagh and at Baislic in the West. This gift of most precious relics signified the exceptional satisfaction of the Holy See with what Patrick had done.

The bond between Ireland and Rome was forged then, which never weakened. As we read the olden literature of Ireland, both Hiberno-Latin and Gaelic, we are struck by the ringing of the name of Rome, Rome, Rome, through it all. The nation which never lay under the yoke of pagan Rome, and that never yielded up its own secular ideals, joyously yielded its loyalty to Rome as Peter's See then, and forever. In the Irish language the very name of Rome, as *Ruam*, became the word for a sacred place, and the consecrated places of the country were called the Romes of Ireland.

From this date of 441, Patricius the Bishop is Metropolitan of Ireland as an ecclesiastical province.

2. CHURCH ORGANISATION

Already, and in the year before the historic retreat on Croagh Patrick, the superiors of the mission in Gaul had manifested their recognition of the Bishop's achievement. In the year 439, three eminent churchmen were sent from Gaul to join Patrick as assistant bishops. These we know as St. Secundinus, St. Auxilius, and St. Iserninus. The first is said to have been Patrick's nephew, but, as he was of much the same age as Patrick, this is hardly likely to be true. The others had been fellow monks with Patrick at Auxerre.

Secundinus was regarded by the old Irish historians as second only to the Apostle himself. Patrick's remarkable personality so dominates the story of the mission that the importance of the work done by his helpers has become obscured; but there can be no doubt that these eminent three made a weighty contribution to the work as organisers, teachers, scholars. How the old Irish esteemed Secundinus is seen by the adoption of his name, in Irish *Seachnall*. The name *Maelseachlainn*, borne by the High-King celebrated in Tom Moore's song as Malachi, who

> ...*wore the collar of gold*
> *Which he won from the proud invader—*

means Client of Seachnall, or of Secundinus. The patronymic of O'Melaghlin, borne by one of the five families whom Anglo-Norman law recognised as royal, has the same origin. Secundinus had his See at the place in Meath which we call Dunshaughlin, famous in the ballad of '98:

> *The Yeos were in Dunshaughlin,*
> *The Hessians in Drumree—*

and the original Irish in *Domhnach Seachlainn*. Thus, in some of the most famous names in Irish history, the memory of the Gallic or Lombard Bishop is enshrined or, as we may say, fossilised.

The name of the second of the three foreign bishops, Auxilius, is embodied in the same fashion in Killossy, where Auxilius had his See, near Naas in what was North Leinster. Iserninus was established some hours' journey from Rathvilly in South Leinster.

For his own primatial See, Patrick chose Armagh, away in Ulster. Why did he not set up his See in Tara of Meath, the High-King's capital? Why did he place his chief assistant not at Tara, but at Dunshaughlin? This place is best known today as a centre for the meeting of the hunt and as a landmark for travellers when seeking their way to the featureless green hill which once was the abode of kings; it is several miles from Tara. Some will say that, as King Laoghaire had refused to be converted, Tara remained a pagan site. MacNeill reasons thus, and adds that Patrick set up his assistants' Sees near to Tara and to the former provincial capitals at Naas and Rathvilly, in accordance with the policy of Continental churchmen to identify the location of secular and spiritual rule. To us the answer seems different.

Observe that Patrick established the most important See of all at a place remote from the centre of political power. Armagh, as we will find a little later, had been a political centre of great importance down to a hundred years before Patrick's mission; and then it had been desolated, when the Kingdom of the Ulidians was overthrown. Patrick thus chose, as it were, a political wilderness as the site for his own headquarters. In like manner, he set up the important Missionary base at Donaghpatrick to the north of Tara, and the See of Secundinus at Dunshaughlin to the south, but neither in the royal city. He wished to be strongly based in Meath, but yet, as it were, aloof from the State. In fine, it seems to us that Patrick's policy, owing to his feeling that a new age needed new methods, was deliberately different from what was usual on the Continent.

Instead of establishing the Church in political capitals, he set it up at a friendly distance. It was as if he said to the kings of the land that he was evangelising: "Do your secular work and let me do mine, which is spiritual. Let us not confound the throne of Caesar with that of God's Bishop." There never was a dispute over Investitures in Irish Christendom.

There is another thing to be noticed in the matter of the Sees which St. Patrick set up. The political system in Ireland was altogether different from that of the empire or of the kingdoms into which the empire dissolved. There were in Ireland no large cities; and those urban centres which had some importance, such as Tara, had no large resident population and were in fact populous only at times of festival, or when armies were mobilising there. As the Greek civilisation was based on the small, autonomous city-State, the civilisation of olden Ireland was based on the small rural State, and the constitution of the whole country has been described as the United States of Ireland; for the States were grouped in confederations culminating in the national monarchy. The States normally were about half as large as a modern county. The principal men did not live in an urban centre, but resembled large farmers or landed gentry; and one elected from a leading family was king. This description of the system applies strictly to a period later than Patrick; for in his time much of the country was in flux and the great royal House which ruled at Tara as yet had but imperfect control of the island. If the constitution had been as clearly defined and as stable as it was when the *Book of Rights* described it in detail a few centuries later, Patrick probably would have made dioceses coincident with the States, or with groups of the States, and the system could have been summed up as one king, one Bishop. In the unsettled fifth century, the best that Patrick could do was to set up Sees of varying importance and range of territorial authority, according to the condition of the regions in which he established the Church.

Accordingly, many of Patrick's bishops had only tiny areas of jurisdiction, corresponding to tiny secular communities. St. Fiacc of Sletty and St. Cianán of Duleek are examples of convert bishops who had but petty dioceses to rule. A surprisingly large number of bishops is said to have been consecrated—it runs to hundreds. However, research cannot find proof that there were more than forty or fifty Sees.

The Church in Ireland was of necessity a new departure in yet another way. Christianity had been born and had grown in a mighty urban civilisation. With the downfall of the Roman cities under the barbarian invasions, a rustication of life set in throughout the lands which pagan Rome had ruled. Accordingly the western Church was obliged to adapt itself to a new social order. A recent historian of the Church speaks of St. Martin, St. Benedict, and St. Patrick as the three great men whose lives sum up the change.[1] "In St. Martin, Bishop of Tours (375-397) we see the pioneer of the Mission to convert the country folk," he writes, and he goes on to speak of the monasticism of St. Benedict which transformed the invaded and war-harried countryside of the Continent. "Finally," he says, "in St. Patrick we see the first Monk Missioner formed by this new rural Christianity, and he founded not merely monasteries, but a whole people which, in time to come, was to show itself a sanctuary for sanctity and culture. From Catholic Ireland, which is his creation, the light was one day to return to re-enlighten Europe itself."

We behold Patrick and his great assistants, therefore, organising the Church in a wholly rural society and on lines which in

---

1.   Philip Hughes, *A History of the Church*, Volume I.

many ways were strange to the Continental model. The bishops of Irish Sees had to live in little self-supporting rural establishments, which easily developed into monasteries in the following century. Patrick's system for the governance of the Church in Ireland, then, was territorial, but it was modified by the irregular areas in which it operated, and its rural form gave it a monastic bias from the first.

Synods held by Patrick and his three assistants are recorded. Together the Irish Metropolitan and the three signed canons for the regulation of the Church in Ireland. These are printed *in extenso* in Archbishop Healy's *Life and Writings of St. Patrick,* and will be found to deal very largely with the stability of the clergy. Wandering clerics are not to be received. Priests arriving from Britain without full credentials are not to be allowed to officiate. Austere rules are laid down to prevent scandals.

At one time, Iserninus was driven from his See, or into exile, by some secular dispute. Doubtless it was during his absence that a canon of particular interest was signed by Patrick, Secundinus and Auxilius, but by Benignus in place of the exile. This canon laid it down that matters of dispute are to be referred to the See at Armagh; and when disputes continue they are to be carried to the Apostolic See, "that is to the See of the Apostle Peter, having the authority of Rome."

3. ST. SECUNDINUS' HYMN

For some years, it seems, Secundinus occupied the See of Armagh in place of Patrick. Here we come on a mysterious affair, of which various explanations have been put forward. One distinguished historian argues that Patrick was suspended from office soon after

the arrival of the three bishops from Gaul. This is Helena Concannon,[2] who champions the theory (already hinted at by some less
sympathetic authors) that the terrible trial to which Patrick alludes
in his Confession, when his best friends turned against him and
his superiors were displeased with him, occurred, not when the
mission was begun, but at this time. Mrs. Concannon thinks that
fault was founded with Patrick's conduct of the Mission and that he
was superseded at the direction of the Apostolic superiors in Auxerre. He then went to Rome, pleaded his case, was approved and
re-instated. This theory is not favoured by later writers. The Rev.
John Ryan, S.J., points out canonical objections.[3] To us it seems
improbable for a simple reason. Secundinus cannot have superseded Patrick and quarrelled with him even for a short time and
yet have been remembered as a mighty figure in the Mission and
as Patrick's great admirer and dear friend. We are content to suppose that if Patrick retired from the Primacy for a time, yielding
it to Secundinus, it was for some natural reason that has not been
recorded. May not ill-health explain a retirement at the time of
the visit to Rome, which was prolonged until 445, when the next
episode in Patrick's career is recorded?

We leave aside this perplexing question and turn to the most
interesting passage in the story of Secundinus. He was the author
of a curious alphabetical poem of ninety-two lines in somewhat
labouring Latin verse, now known as *The Hymn of Secundinus*. It
is a glowing praise of Patrick. According to Concannon's theory, it
was made on the reconciliation between the two eminent churchmen when Patrick resumed the Primacy. According to an ancient

---

2.   Helena Concannon, *St. Patrick, His Life and Mission*.
3.   John Ryan, S.J., *Irish Monasticism*.

text in Irish, prefixed to the poem itself, it was made as a peace-offering, but after only a trifling moment of vexation. This old account says that Secundinus one day remarked that Patrick had one fault; namely, that he did not preach almsgiving sufficiently.

Hearing this, Patrick was angered. "It is for charity's sake that I do not preach charity," he said; "for if I preached almsgiving, everything would be given to me, and those who follow me would fare poorly."

This sentence alludes, of course, to the well-known fact that Patrick always refused to ask for or even to accept gifts; for it was his purpose to establish the Church and give the faith to Ireland without payment from the people.

The story says that Secundinus knew that he had vexed Patrick by his little criticism and that he composed the poem as a kind of peace-offering. He met Patrick somewhere near Slieve Gullion, and said that he had made a hymn in praise of a certain Son of Life which he wished Patrick to hear.

"The praise of God's household is welcome to me," said Patrick.

Secundinus then read the poem, but omitted the first stanza as Patrick's name appears therein. Patrick admired and praised the anonymous portrait of a good Churchman, and then Secundinus read the first stanza disclosing that it referred to Patrick himself.

Audite, omnes amantes Deum, sancta merita
Viri in Christo beati Patricii Episcopi:
Quomodo bonum ob actum simulatur angelis,
Perfectamque propter vitam aequatur Apostolis.[4]

---

4. "Oh, all ye lovers of God hear the holy merits of the blessed man in Christ, the Bishop Patrick, who by the goodness of his deeds, is like unto the angels, and for the perfection of his life is evened with the Apostles."

The authorship of Secundinus is almost certainly authentic, whatever about the story of a quarrel and a reconciliation; and it is the most ancient document for the Life of Patrick. It describes the Bishop's sanctity and extols his orthodoxy. It is a portrait of the perfect missionary bishop. "Constant in the fear of God and immovable in faith, on whom as on Peter the Church is built; the Lord chose him that he should teach barbarous peoples." Appointed by the Saviour, he is an instructor of the clergy, and a true pastor of souls. "He feeds the faithful with celestial feasts, lest those who are seen in Christ's company should faint by the way: to these he deals out as loaves the words of the Gospel—like manna they are multiplied in his hands." Here we have a manifest allusion to Patrick's notable familiarity with the Scriptures. Beside the sacraments and instructions, Patrick distributes vestments and books. Here we are reminded of the enormous labour which the provision of vestments and altar linen and missals and psalters entailed in those days when hand labour had to supply a rapidly expanding Mission. The Hymn describes Patrick as a ransomer of slaves—and we shall see that this was true of the ex-slave who had become the Irish Primate. It alludes to Patrick's "confirmation in the Catholic faith," clearly referring to the Roman approbation as commemorated in the Annals. It is important to find Patrick already portrayed as a national Apostle. Secundinas recognised his master as the national figure which he was, "like Paul, an Apostle to the Gentiles." Secundinas is believed to be the author also of *Sancti Venite*, the oldest Eucharistic hymn still extant. This beautiful piece certainly comes from Ireland and at latest was composed not much later than Patrick's day; so it quite well may be the work of Secundinas as many believe. The olden Gaelic narrative says that angels were heard singing it around the Blessed Sacrament in the church, on the occasion when the little quarrel between Patrick and Secundinus was healed.

> *Sancti venite,*
> *Christi Corpus sumite;*
> *Sanctum bibentes*
> *Quo redempti sanguinem.*
> *Salvati Christi*
> *Corpore et sanguine,*
> *A quo refecti*
> *Laudes dicamus Deo.*
> *Hoc sacramento*
> *Corporis et sanguinis,*
> *Omnes exuti*
> *Ab inferni faucibus.*

"Come, O ye holy ones, receive the Body of Christ and drink that Holy Blood by which you are redeemed;

"By Christ's Body saved and by His Blood refreshed, let us sing praises unto God;

"By this Sacrament of the Body and Blood, from the fangs of hell are all drawn back..."

This poem, dating from Patrician days, was intoned as an antiphon at Bangor in later days, when the Abbot and his priests received communion. If it was not written actually by Patrick's chief assistant, at least it shows us what manner of men were those first clergy of Ireland, and that devotion to the Blessed Sacrament was conspicuous from the earliest days of the Irish Church.

4. The Church of Martyrs

We have seen that Patrick received relics of the Apostles in Rome in 441. He enshrined them in Armagh in 444 or 445, and that date is reckoned as the foundation of the Primatial City.

Today, Armagh, with some seven thousand inhabitants, is half Cathedral city, half market town. It is little, quiet, fragrant as a dairy and dignified as a library; a homely, yet historic and enchanting place. The town is built on two hills, crowned by ecclesiastical buildings. The Catholic cathedral, with twin spires that are landmarks to a vast region of pleasant farm-land and orchard country, stands on the second hill-top, and outside the olden bounds of the Cathedral city. The Protestant cathedral occupies the summit of the main hill, and is on the site of the Catholic cathedral of other times. Round this summit, there are two concentric circles of streets, built where vast concentric ramparts once guarded the hill-top. The eye at once discovers that ancient Armagh was a fortified place.

Two miles to the west, there are vast green ramparts in the fields, making the site of Emania, the primeval stronghold of kings. Here we can realise the immensity of the ancient power. Hundreds of years before Christ, toiling multitudes dug the circular trenches and raised the earthen ramparts, to make an impregnable city. When Augustus ruled the Roman world, Conchobhar mac Nessa was monarch here; and Athairne, the king's poet, wore the cloak of swan's plumage which signified his primacy in his art, when Virgil in Rome was chapleted with laurel. Here the great house, named the Red Branch, was filled with the warriors of the Irish Iliad, Cuchulainn and Conall Cearnach and the Sons of Usnagh and the rest, and here Deirdre the beautiful, whom the poets afterwards named with Helen, came to her tragic doom. In the year 332, of

the Christian era—exactly a century before Patrick's mission—
Emania was overthrown and sacked. The Three Collas, nephews of
the High-King of that time, swept into the northern stronghold to
humble its rulers and destroy a power that rivalled Tara. Eastward
the remnants of the defeated power retreated, to entrench what we
call Down and Armagh as the Kingdom of Ulidia; but Emania's
royal houses lay in ruins, within those green ramparts which we
still may climb.

In Patrick's time, therefore, Emania was but a long-gutted fortress, a place of no living consequences. A small chieftain named
Dáire dwelt there, lord of that forsaken countryside.

Hither came the Bishop. What caused him to come to Emania
and the neighbouring Armagh is not known. It is recorded that he
had planned to set up his See at Louth, in the kindly green farming country, thirty miles to the south. Beside the little country village of Louth there is a hill named Ardpatrick, with ecclesiastical
remains; a place doubly sacred because a successor of Patrick, the
outlawed Primate, Blessed Oliver Plunkett, lived here in hiding in
the Penal days. When pilgrims climb the gentle eminence of Ardpatrick, a guide points to a thicket on the summit and tells how the
people say that Patrick stood at this point and looked northward to
the mountains of Ulster (a fair sight on the skyline), as he took his
decision to go to Armagh. Ancient writers say that Patrick's angel
inspired him, when he was at Louth, to make the fateful change in
his purpose; he left St. Mochta, one of his helpers from Britain, in
Louth.

Northward, then, he pierced the highland country and came
to Emania and the Height of Macha. Can it be that it came into his
mind that accommodation could be got easily at a deserted site,
just as missions in our own day have taken up and transformed the

deserted mansions and demesnes of the fallen landlords?

The Bishop went to Dáire's *dún*, or ramparted dwelling, beside Emania and asked for a site for his church.

"What place do you desire?" Dáire inquired: his actual words are recorded.

"I wish," said Patrick, "to get the high ground, called the Ridge of the Willows"—signifying the central hill of the modern city.

It seems reasonable to suppose that, while Dáire occupied Emania, the neighbouring height, with its double ramparts, once a barrack of the Ulidian forces, lay empty and to a petty lord useless. However, Dáire grudged the splendid site and replied:

"I will not give you the Ridge of the Willows, but I will give you a site for your church in the lower ground."

Patrick accepted the gift, and built his first church there, "close to Armagh," to dwell there with his community for many years.

This was in the year 444 or 445. The church which Patrick then built was known as *Fertae Martyrum* in Latin, or *Na ferta* in Irish, signifying the Church of the Martyrs. This name was given because Patrick enshrined here the relics which he had received from Pope St. Leo; and olden records tell how the relics were venerated with vigils and lights, psalm-singing by day and prayer at night and annual exposition. Every Sunday, in later days, there was a procession from the Height of Armagh to the Church of the Relics, the worshippers singing the psalm, *Domine clamavi.*

For the present, however, the height of Armagh was not ceded to the Bishop. Not until thirteen years afterwards, when the aged Metropolitan was about to end his laborious career, was the hill made his and his great stone church built, in a way of which we will tell later.

CHAPTER X

Labour and Triumph

1. THE PREACHER

As the life-story of the Apostle of Ireland proceeds, it becomes dim and confused. Legends crowd upon the biographer, and he finds it hard to detach the likely truth from evident fable. The Roman approbation of 441 stands clear, and the foundation of Armagh as the Metropolitan See in 444 or 445. After that, the distinctness with which we have been able to visualise the youth, the call, and the first victories of the mission fails until, as we shall see, the last years of the Apostle's life, from 457 to 461, which he spent in retirement, are suddenly illuminated by his own writings. For the period between 445 and 457 we have no chronological record. It is a period teeming with activity, in which the triumphant mission was carried far and wide through the island, but we cannot trace the development of events in sequence. We hear of journeys through Leinster and Munster, and some accounts speak of a circuit of Ireland. We are not to suppose that Patrick was continually in motion; he was Metropolitan now, with assistants who carried on the work of evangelisation and organisation. Much of his time was spent in Armagh. Yet the stories of wondrous deeds and adventures, so numerous that there is hardly a region in Ireland without its Patrician legends, prove a tireless activity, and indeed, the saint's own words are ample evidence. Summing up what we must wish that he had described in detail, he says: "It was necessary to spread our nets widely." He tells how he travelled "through many perils even in remote parts where no man dwelt," and speaks of twelve perils, many ambushes and plots, and at least one capture of his whole company, with intent to murder.

We are obliged to treat these obscure, though eventful, years, in an episodic manner. In 447, Secundinus died, at the age of seventy-five, while Patrick was in his early sixties. We are left to conjecture how largely Secundinus prepared the harvest that Patrick reaped in Leinster; for though the Tripartite Life, and other narratives written in Patrick's honour, represent him as the first evangelist of every place that he visited, it is plain that his assistants must have done a large part of the immense work, so that the journeys through the South-East and South which he made after the death of his chief coadjutor may have been in the nature of a triumphant progress through land that had been well prepared by his fellow-labourers. On those journeys, he carried relics of the Martyrs with him. He consecrated churches, visited kings, and preached to eager crowds. Though it is true that large areas were pagan even at his life's end, it is certain that the greater part of the island was converted in his days. The adhesion in mass of large populations to the Christian faith may be attributed to that trait of the Gaelic people which we call clannishness; that is, a certain unanimity of public opinion, moving with its leaders. We see this quality in a period which stands in the full light of history when the Gaels of Scotland, in the different highland territories, went with their Chiefs, some for the Reformation and the new system, some for the old faith and the national cause. In Patrick's age, the intense unison of mind must have aided the work of conversion from paganism to Christianity. A prince received the Apostle favourably, and opinion set for the Christian cause in a swift, decided movement; minds turned together to the faith with a unanimity like that of the birds of the air that we see wheel about instantly, as if moved by a single will.

Patrick is recorded to have been a marvellous preacher. Indeed, his ardent, irascible, intrepid nature, so evident in his writings and in all the characteristic stories of him, make it easy to imagine how he would pour forth the abundance of his love of God, his indignation against wrong, his zeal for souls, in addresses that carried his hearers with him. We can imagine him preaching to multitudes in the manner of Father Matthew, the Capuchin apostle of temperance, whose progress through Ireland in the last century was one long series of monster meetings, as the people crowded forth eagerly to drink his holy words and to answer his appeal to mortification. Immediately after Catholic Emancipation in 1829, Rosminian Fathers came to Ireland to preach the first missions since the Penal age, and whole countrysides hosted to hear the preachers. In big fields, thousands would camp to hear sermons and receive the sacraments. Recall also the huge city congregations which mustered to hear that master of sacred eloquence, the Dominican Father Burke, or the Jesuit Fathers of Dublin in the century of the Irish Church's second Spring. Just such responsiveness must have aided the swift conversion of territories fifteen centuries ago.

We have actual examples of Patrick's sacred eloquence in his address to the maidens at the Well of Clebach, and again in his Confession. He was preaching, remember, to people whose religion hitherto was a worship of Nature, fostered by Druids who were poets and who taught their hearers to see the Supernatural in the splendour of the sun. We find a passage in Patrick's Confession, concerning the sun of Nature, and God who made that sun, which exalts us by its beauty as we read, and which must be an authentic example of his preaching.

"That sun, which we see, by God's command rises daily for our benefit; but it never will reign, nor will its splendour endure; but all those who worship it will pass through wretched misery to punishment; we, however, believe in and adore the true Sun, which is Christ, who never shall perish, and neither shall anyone who does His will, but he shall live unto eternity, even as Christ, who reigneth with God the Father Almighty and with the Holy Spirit before all ages, now and for evermore.... For without any doubt soever, we shall rise on that day in the brightness of the Sun, that is, of Christ Jesus our Redeemer, as sons of the living God and co-heirs with Christ and conformed to His future likeness; for of Him and through Him and in Him are all things. To Him be glory forever and ever, Amen; for in Him we shall reign."

These words Patrick wrote to be read by people of the land that his mission was converting; they show us that thoughts were in his mind during that mission. If he wrote thus, he must have spoken thus. Conceive those words, therefore, as delivered in a sermon—poured forth in molten Gaelic by that commanding figure, so manly, so stately, and yet so homely—and consider how they must appeal to listeners who had been trained to that sublime but unsatisfying thing which is Nature-worship. The teaching of Druids and poets had gone just as far as Natural religion can; it had created the appetite for the supernatural which Patrick now satisfied with the Bread of Life.

He used to preach at extraordinary length. One very old and curious story tells that the Bishop's sermon once lasted for three days. A young woman in the entranced audience fell asleep, and

Patrick would not let her be wakened; but, at the end of that remarkable discourse, the sleeper woke. She was Brigid, who as yet was too young to be a nun. Patrick asked her what she had seen in her dream. She replied:

"I beheld four ploughs in the north-east which ploughed the whole island, and before the sowing was finished the harvest was ripened and clear well-springs and shiny streams came out of the furrows. White garments were on the sowers and ploughmen.

"I also beheld four other ploughs in the north which ploughed the island athwart and turned the harvest again, and the oats which they had sown grew up at once and were ripe, and black streams came out of the furrows, and there were black garments on the sowers and on the ploughmen."

This curious vision Patrick explained to Brigid thus:

The first four ploughs which you saw, those are you and I, who sow the four books of the Gospel with a sowing of faith and belief and piety. The harvest which you saw are they who come unto that faith and belief through our teaching.

The four ploughs which you beheld in the north are the false teachers and the liars who will overturn the teaching which we have sown.

Brigid was a young girl when Patrick was nearing the end of his labours, so this meeting may be no legend, but a fact. That vigorous young spirit would be eager to meet the Apostle who had won most of Ireland for the faith.

2. Friends and Unfriends

Such was the Apostle's progress, where it was most favourable. Yet, even in those days when men knew that Ireland was won for the faith, he often met opposition and persecution. Jealous men often endangered his life. He came into Offaly, on one of his journeys through Leinster. One of the principal men in that region boasted that he would kill Patrick if he should meet him, in revenge for the destruction of Cromm Cruach, the idol god of Magh Sleacht. Now, Patrick's charioteer, Odhrán, was an Offaly man; he knew of the threat, and with Patrick's household concealed it from the Bishop.

One day Odhrán said to Patrick (here we follow the Tripartite Life): "Since I am driving the chariot for you a long time, Father Patrick (a bhoba Pátraic), let me sit in the chief seat today."

Patrick agreed; and the would-be murderer of the Bishop cast his spear at the seated figure and slew the faithful servant.

This happened at Killeigh, near Tullamore. The name Odhrán, by the way, signifies dun-coloured; it was borne subsequently by nine Irish saints, one of whom was patron of Waterford, and one of whom we shall meet in the story of St. Columcille.

Murder could be attempted in this cowardly manner, but the mission could not be publicly opposed, such was its prestige in the land, and the protection which it enjoyed from the highest authority. Where the ex-slave wished to go, his intrepidity earned him. He still began, where possible, with the conversion of rulers. At Naas, the old North Leinster capital, two princes received baptism from the Apostle, and their sisters entered religion. At Rathvilly, farther south, the lord of the region was baptised at Patrick's hands in the river which flows today just before a Catholic church in which the incident is depicted above the chancel arch and country folk are reminded at every Mass that they kneel where the Apostle of Ireland converted a king.

Who has not heard the moving story of Angus, King of Cashel—the rock capital of all Munster—who with numbers of his people received the faith? On that sublime, regal eminence in the midst of the Golden Vale of Tipperary, commanding a view that is circled by distant, lovely mountains, while Cormac's Romanesque chapel, a cathedral and a castle and many high crosses are crowded above us like the spurs of a crown, we still may see the stone on which the kings of Munster were inaugurated in those distant days. On the morning when Patrick arrived at Cashel, "all the idols were on their faces," the old Life says—signifying, perhaps, that the people of Cashel flung down the pagan emblems in preparation for the Apostle's coming. Many folk, headed by Angus, the king, and his brothers, were baptised there, on the royal height.

As he baptised Angus, Patrick inadvertently thrust the spike of his crozier through the King's foot. Angus gave no sign. He endured the agony of transfixion while the prayers were said and the ceremony completed.

"Why did you not tell me of this mistake?"—Patrick asked, when he discovered what had happened.

"I thought it was part of the ritual," Angus simply replied.

In reward, it is said, Patrick promised Angus that none of his descendants should die of wounds. He blessed Cashel; and we read that he celebrated Mass on every seventh ridge of that happy journey through the South.

He did not go into Thomond (which we now call Clare), but he stayed for a space at Limerick, and he uttered blessings on the territory about the Shannon, and the isles. "The men of Thomond came southward in sea-fleets to meet Patrick, and he baptised

them at Tirglass." This ancient record enables us to see the men
of Clare—that race of big-bodied, ever Irish-hearted folk; the race
that smashed the Penal code when Daniel O Connell fought his
Ennis election—hosting by water to Limerick to hear the famous
preacher, and being baptised in a multitude at the place, Tírglass,
now called Patrick's Well, three miles south of the present Limerick city. There, too, the name of Donaghmore commemorates the
church that Patrick founded in this place.

Ere he left Munster, Patrick blessed a feast, which was given by
Bishop Trian, "a pilgrim of the Romans," we are told; and then he
bade farewell to men of Munster and blessed them. The happiness
of those days in the South, days of welcome and of holy joy, comes
to us across the centuries, when we read the Gaelic verses which
were made to perpetuate Patrick's words as, with an overflowing
heart, he said:

> Bennacht for firu Muman
> Feraib, maccaib, mnáib....
> *Blessing on the men of Munster,*
> *Men, young folk, women;*
> *Blessing on the land*
> *That yields its fruit to them.*
> *Blessing on every treasure*
> *That shall be gathered on their plains,*
> *Without anyone in want of help—*
> *God's blessing on Munster.*
> *Blessing on their peaks*
> *And on their bare flagstones,*
> *Blessing on their glens,*
> *Blessing on their ridges.*

As sea-sand under ships
Be the number of their hearths,
On slopes, on plains,
On moors, on mountains.

3. The Laws of Ireland

The protection of the High-King Laoghaire, so helpful in the first years of the mission, must have followed Patrick all his days. Though the pagan monarch refused the faith, he well may have grown ever friendlier with time. His son Conall, and his daughters had become Patrick's converts, and he must have regarded the new religion with ever more indulgent eyes as he saw it moulding the land in the ways of peace and culture. Patrick's missionary career coincided in time almost exactly with the king's reign. Laoghaire had been two years High-King when Patrick landed in 432, and he fell in battle in 462, just a year after the Apostle's death. We may regard the rapid conversion of the people partly as cause and partly as effect of the official friendliness to the extension of the Church in Ireland, and this friendliness was signalised, probably in Patrick's last and triumphant years, by a remarkable event. An old account says that Laoghaire undertook the codification of the civil laws, invited Patrick's aid, and caused the work to be carried out by a joint commission of nine, comprising three kings: the High-King Laoghaire and a king from the North and a king from the South; three bishops: Patrick and Benignus and Cairnech; and three scholars of the native learning: Dubthach mac Lugair and two others.

This story of a joint commission of Church and State is

considered fabulous. At that time, the writing of Gaelic, save in
monumental inscriptions, had not begun, and the brehons preserved the laws, like the historic records, by marvellous feats of
memory—the mnemonic feats of the Druids of Gaul were noted
by Caesar five hundred years earlier. Yet, though the writing of the
Gaelic tongue for literary purposes did not begin for another two
centuries, and the oldest fragments of Irish written law date from
the seventh century at the earliest, it is certain that some notable
conference between Patrick and Laoghaire, touching the civil law,
took place. In the early years of Laoghaire's reign in Ireland, the
Emperor Theodosius published in Byzantium the *Codex* which
bears his name, a great statement of the laws of the empire. It well
may be that Laoghaire desired to copy the ruler of the Roman world
in this, and to codify the laws of Ireland, just as other High-Kings
had copied the empire in fortifications and military roads and a
standing army. Yet more likely, the initiative was with Patrick. He
may have desired of the High-King that the civil law should be
revised in order to satisfy the growing Christian community.

The oldest Irish law-tract,[1] dating from the seventh century,
records in a somewhat cryptic manner this adjustment of the civil
law to the Christian requirements. It tells how Laoghaire, at the
time of Patrick's first coming to Tara, was moved to oppose him
by the Druid Matha, son of Urnor, who warned the High-King
that the Christian would steal the living and the dead from him.
Said Matha of Patrick: "He will free slaves, he will exalt kins of low
degree through the grades of the Church and the service of repen-
tance to God; for the Kingdom of heaven is open to every kindred
of men who have believed, alike to the free and the unfree; even so

---

1.   A. S. Green, *The Irish State to 1014.*

the Church is open before every man, whosoever cometh under her government."

Laoghaire's opposition was broken down at the very outset, however, by the conversion of Dubthach mac Lugair, the poet who was Patrick's first convert at Tara; for this eminent poet, being of the druidic caste, negatived the influence of Matha. In other words, the party among the native scholars which was favourable to the faith prevailed over that which was hostile, and Laoghaire's influence was decisive.

"The Law of Nature it was that the men of Ireland had until the coming of the faith in the time of Laoghaire," says the ancient law tract. "When the men of Ireland accepted the faith from Patrick, the two laws were combined, the Law of Nature and the Law of Scripture. Dubthach mac Lugair the poet expounded to Patrick the Law of Nature—he who was first to stand up to receive him at Tara."

Every three years, the great *Feis*, or Assembly, of Tara was the occasion for law-making or revision. It seems that at one *Feis*, the reconciliation of native law to Christian demands was carried out. The account on which we here rely, in preference to that which speaks of a commission, attributes the work to Dubthach and Patrick. As there is other evidence of Dubthach acting as Patrick's trusted adviser, a prolonged friendship and co-operation seems credible enough, and we assign this harmonising of the laws to a late period in Patrick's life.

"Dubthach declared the law-rules of the Men of Ireland," the old tract says. "Many things which they had reached in the Law of Nature, but which the Law of Scripture had not reached, Dubthach also showed to Patrick. That which did not conflict with the Word of God and the conscience of the faithful, Dubthach and Patrick combined in the system of the jurists for the Church and the men of Irish learning. The whole Law of Nature had been right save the faith and its dues and the harmony of Church with State and the dues of each from and towards the other; for," the tract says in a remarkable sentence, "there is the due of the State towards the Church and the due of the Church towards the State."

It is recorded that Patrick's influence on the secular law was to modify many severities in favour of the common folk. He secured many exemptions from taxation, many rights which enlarged the liberty of the person. "Patrick's influence must have gone far," Mrs. A. S. Green observes,[2] "before he could even be supposed to touch the sacred fabric of ancient custom; and the unknown jurist bears a fine testimony to the reputed understanding tolerance and wisdom of the Apostle as preserved in the learned tradition of the law. The memory of his protection of the common folk survived through later centuries in the solemnity and popular emotion with which the reliquary of the saint was carried before the king's seat at Tailtiu, for the more solemn administration of oaths in some grave case of law."

The ex-slave was the people's advocate as well as their apostle.

4. THE HOUSEHOLD OF PATRICK

What other story shall we tell of Patrick's deeds? We might cite an anecdote concerning almost every one of his household, who are listed in the Tripartite Life thus:

---

2.   Ibid.

Sechnall, his bishop.

Mochta, his priest.

Bishop Ere, his judge.

Bishop MacCairthinn, his champion.

Benen, his psalmist.

Coeman of Cell Riada, his chamberlain.

Sinell of Cell Dareis, his bell-ringer.

Athcen of Both Domnaig, his cook.

Presbyter Mescan of Domnach Mescain at Fochain, his brewer.

Presbyter Catan and Presbyter Acan, his two attendants at table.

Odhrán of Disert Odrain in Hui Failgi, his charioteer.

Presbyter Manach, his fire-woodman.

Rottan, his cowherd.

His three smiths, namely, Macc Cecht; (Laeban) of Domnach Laebain, who made the (bell called) Findfaidech, and Fortchern in Rath Adine—or, as it is elsewhere, Rath Semni.

His three wrights, Essa, and Bite, and Tassach.

His three embroideresses, Lupait, and Ere, daughter of Daire, and Cruimtheris in Cengoba.

He had also three masons, not given here, namely, Caeman, Cruineach, and Luireach the Strong.

Of these, Sechnall or Seachnall is familiar to us already; he is described here as Patrick's bishop, signifying his coadjutor. Mochta is the Briton whom Patrick established in Louth. Bishop Ere is that lawyer who was converted at the outset of the mission and became bishop of Slane. We have met Benen, or Benignus, and Odhrán,

too. Bishop MacCairthinn, Patrick's "champion," is the patron of
the diocese of Clogher, and the playful fable is dear to Monaghan
men which tells how MacCairthinn carried Patrick over the
flooded river and threatened to set him down in the midst of the
waters if he would not grant him the bishopric of that place. The
Tripartite Life gives another account.

Once, as Patrick was coming from Clogher out of the North,
his champion (*trenfer*, i.e., strong man), Mac-Cairthinn, lifted him
over a difficult place. This is what he said after lifting Patrick: "Oh,
oh!"

"*Mo Dé broth!*" says Patrick, "it was not usual for you to utter
that word."

"I am now an old man and I am infirm," says Mac-Cairthinn,
"and you have left my comrades in churches, but I am still on the
road."

"I will leave you, then, in a church," said Patrick; and he added
that it should be a church not so near to Armagh that they would
be tempted to much visiting, nor yet so far that visiting should be
impossible. So Mac-Cairthinn got Clogher, a day's journey from
Armagh.

Nothing seems too small to remember about Patrick; for there
was character in all his words and acts. Even his exclamation when
vexed, "*Mo Dé broth!*" is recorded. No one is sure what the expression means, although Dr. Osborn Bergin explains it as a phrase of
Old Welsh, *min doiu braut*, meaning: "By the God of Judgment!"
The saint grows homelier to us when we know what explosive word
he used to rebuke blunderers or sluggards or contrary people.

The exclamation comes into many of the anecdotes of the Apostle told in the Tripartite Life. Once a blind man went to encounter Patrick, and hurriedly poured out his tale of woe. Someone in

Patrick's household laughed at the poor fellow.

"*Mo Dé broth!*" cried Patrick, "it would be fitting if you were the blind man!"—and the story goes that the blind man was healed, while the mocker lost his sight.

At some place in Mayo or Sligo certain heathen folk flung stones at the Bishop and his company. "*Mo Dé broth!*"—said Patrick; "in every contest, you shall be defeated, and in every conference despised!"

At Naas, in Leinster, Patrick summoned an official of the royal dún; but the unhelpful fellow feigned sleep. When Patrick was told that the man was sleeping, he exclaimed: "*Mo Dé broth!*—I would not wonder if this were his last sleep!"—and so it proved.

At Drumboe, Patrick was resting on Sunday and slept, but a great noise by pagan folk who were digging a rath disturbed him. He asked the men to be quiet, but they ridiculed him. "*Mo Dé broth!*"—cried Patrick, "may your toil not prosper!"—and next night a wind from the sea destroyed the work.

Certain of the people of Omeath stole and ate two of Patrick's goats and denied the theft; but the eaten goat bleated within them—so the story tells. "*Mo Dé broth!*"—said Patrick, "the goat himself betrays you." To this odd story it may be added that the supposed descendants of the goat-stealers are pointed at, in a certain townland, to the present day, and the taunt often is uttered in jest: "Who stole St. Patrick's goat?"

He even used his favourite exclamation when he talked with angels, according to one story. The old writers preserved the unusual expression, perhaps because it was strange to Gaelic ears, and perhaps because it enabled them to understand the driving energy of this remarkable man. Can we not imagine the caravan's journey across rough Connacht more easily, when we think of the missionary crying to his slack workers: "*Mo Dé broth!*—do you think we have till Christmas to reach Cruachain?"

Among tales which illustrate Patrick's methods is that which tells how he was walking with some of his neophytes, who carried staves on which letters were written or cut, learning the Latin alphabet as they went. Certain pagans mistook the company of scholars for a force armed with swords, and prepared to attack them—so much the staves resembled weapons. Thus did Patrick infuse his own energy into his disciples, that even on the march they improved their time with study!

A relic of the saint which was preserved in after times in the West, was a tooth, which the possessors encased in a shrine of wood, crystal, precious stones and amber, called *Fiacal Phadraig*. Of this tooth a homely tale is told. Patrick began to lose his teeth in later life, and these were preserved by his friends as mementoes; in time, they even gave names to churches, like *Cill Fiacail*, the Church of the Tooth, near Tipperary town. When Patrick was on a visitation to North Connacht, he erected a church in what now is the parish of Killespugbrone, "the Church of Bishop Brón." While sojourning there, he lost a tooth and Bishop Brón preserved it: that is the tooth for which the handsome shrine was made in later times.

From these tales, which seem to be founded on fact, let us turn to legendary narrative, to see what image of Patrick was held by the poetic traditions of that richly hued, rural, Gaelic world, into which his clear-cut Roman beginnings pass and are transformed.

CHAPTER XI

The Traditional Portrait

1. Old Soldiers' Tales

The traditional conception of the Apostle of Ireland, as we find it in Gaelic literature and folklore, bears witness to the identical character which we have traced in historic fact. He appears as a dominating figure at once strange to Ireland and yet Irish of the Irish, inasmuch as he devotes himself to Ireland, is completely accepted, and becomes one with the land of his adoption as man and wife are one. The vehemence and the gentleness, the force and the humility, so conspicuous in the historic Patrick are the marks of the Pádraig mac Calpuirn of the Gaelic imagination.

About the end of the twelfth century, in an age when Gaelic literature was at one of its brilliant periods, a work entitled *Agallamh na Seanorach*, "The Colloquy of the Ancients," was composed—the second longest prose text in classical Gaelic letters.[1] In vivid and romantic tones it depicts Patrick's circuit of Ireland, and tells how

---

1. Standish H. O'Grady, *Silva Cadelica*. This work contains text and translation of the Colloquy. The text alone has been edited also by Stokes and Windisch (*Irische Texte*). Extracts of translation will be found in *Ancient Irish Tales*, edited by T. P. Cross and C. H. Sloven. See also De Blacam: *Gaelic Literature Surveyed*.

the last heroes of the Fianna Eireann encounter him and become his companions. From place to place, the Roman cleric and the gigantic huntsmen-warriors go together; and as Patrick consecrates a church, the Fenian tells him the story of some marvellous deed of ancient days, transacted at that spot. Now the story makes Caoilte and Oisin (Ossian), who flourished two centuries earlier, the heroes who come to Patrick, so that the whole framework of the work seems fabulous. Yet there may be some authenticity in it, in this way. While the Fenians were in their hey-day as a national militia under Cormac mac Airt, that great organiser, in the third century, and the legends of Caoilte and Oisin the son of Fionn belong to that age, yet the institution of Fenian bands, serving the kings, continued down to the days of Niall. Fenian hosts were they who joined the Picts in the continual attacks on the Roman Wall, and Fenian forces were those that Niall mobilised when he invaded Britain and the boy Patricius was captured. The Fenians pass from history in the days of Laoghaire, who was as peaceful as his father Niall was warlike. Hence, there must have been many old warriors living when Patrick laboured in Laoghaire's reign, their occupation gone, and many of them full of old soldiers' tales such as the Colloquy contains. Saints and soldiers make the best of friends— over in the Holy Land, in Patrick's age, St. Jerome used to describe his own monastic life in soldiers' terms: *Hierosolymam militaturus pergerem*—and we can be sure that many an old Fenian was among Patrick's converts and strongest admirers.

Therefore, we think it likely that the Colloquy was suggested by some tradition of friendship between the Apostle and Fenian converts; after the lapse of centuries, the author (whose identity is unknown) took the artistic liberty of making the survivors of Niall's Fenians into impossible survivors from the age of Cormac and Fionn. Let us bear in mind that an old soldier of such-and-such a disbanded regiment today, if he told stories of the wars to a foreign ecclesiastic, well might include tales of victories won by his regiment before ever he carried arms; telescoping them into the story of his own lifetime.

The "Colloquy" tells that Patrick and his company were at Rath Drumderg—possibly Rathdrum in County Wicklow, that lovely town on golden rocks high above the river that glitters through the wooded vale of Clara—when some old Fenians, out of retirement, drew near.

"Patrick was chanting the sacred Canon (of the Mass), and praising the Creator, and blessing the rath where Fionn, son of Cual, once had been. The clerics saw Caoilte and his band draw near; and fear fell upon them before the big men with their huge hounds—for they were not folk of one epoch with them. Then did that princely one, that pillar of dignity and earthly angel, Patrick mac Calpuirn, the apostle of the Gaels, rise up, and he took the aspergillum to shake holy water on the big men; for until that day a thousand legions of demons had been over them, but now the demons fled into the hills and the scraps and the uttermost limits of the land, and then the big men sat down.

"'Well, my dear child,' said Patrick, 'and what is your name?'

"'Caoilte mac Rónáin,' said he.

"For a long space the clerics gazed and marvelled; for the largest man among the clergy barely reached to the waist or the shoulder of the warriors....

"'Well,' said Patrick, 'have our provisions come yet?'

"'They have,' said the Bishop Seachnall (Secundinus).

"'Distribute the food,' Patrick said, 'and give half to those nine big warriors of the remnants of the Fianna.'

"Then his bishops and his priests and his psalmodists rose and they blessed the food and they all took their fill of food and ale, in the measure fitting for their souls' welfare."

2. SAINT AND FENIAN

This ceremonial feast of welcome being finished, Patrick began to question Caoilte concerning the days of old.

Was not Fionn, the Fenian chief, a good lord?—to which question a famous answer was given in verse:

> *Dámadh ór an duille donn*
> Were the autumn leaves of gold
> That fall upon the forest floor,
> Did the foaming ocean wave
> Break in silver on the shore,
> Fionn would give it all away
> And wish that it were more.

"What virtues upheld you in your lives?" the Bishop asked, and Caoilte made another famous answer, a summary of the natural virtues: "Truth in our hearts, strength in our hands, fulfilment in our tongues."

In reply to question after question, Caoilte described the olden Fenian hunts and the hounds and the horses; he named, also, the chief men and praised Oisin in particular. "Never did Oisin deny any man, in matter of gold or silver or food, nor yet did he ask aught of any, though he were as rich as a king."

"Win victory and blessing, Caoilte," said Patrick; "all this delights our mind and spirit, were it not a loss of devotion and distraction from prayer."

Again he asked where the Fianna found the best hunting, whether in Ireland or Scotland, and Caoilte answered Arran, and recited a poem in praise of that high-peaked island between the two lands; a poem which is almost the loveliest Nature poem in the Gaelic, *Arann na naigheadh niomdha.*

This specially delighted the saint. "For the future," said he, "your stories and yourself are dear to us."

On goes the narrative, enchanting us into that world dear to the Gaelic imagination of princes who are huntsmen and huntsmen who are poets; we can smell the wind on the heather under the summer's sun, and we find charm in the background of Nature to every royal scene. Sometimes Patrick sits in his tent, after toil, to hear stories in the cool of the evening; sometimes it is on the lawn of Tara that the tales are told. We are brought to Elphin (one of the Sees that Patrick founded), and behold, the old Fenian who explains the place-names tells that it was formerly *Ros-na-h Eachraidhe*, the Wood of the Horses; for, says Caoilte, when the nobles of Erin would be feasting at Cruachain of the West, it is there that they would stable their horses in herb-gardens. "Well, well, Caoilte," says Patrick, "you have no end of information." There is a sly touch in this comment, and when one of the Fenian stories of olden conflict tells of love-affairs gone awry, Patrick observes that romances as a rule are indeed involved affairs—*Gabhlánach an rud an scéalaigheacht.* Thus is the humour of the Gael woven into the varied picture, and we feel the spell that is supposed to cause the saint many scruples. Is he doing right to attend to so much secular lore and poetry? He retires in prayer and asks his two angels-of-special-protection (*dhá aingel fhor-coimhéat*) whether it is the will of heaven's King that he should be listening to the Fenian tales. "With one voice and concordantly the angels answered: 'O holy and beloved cleric, know that not more than one third of the Fenian tales live in those old soldiers' memory; and let you have them written down on poets' tablets and in scholars' words, for it will be a delight to companies of worthy people to listen to those tales even to time's end.'" Patrick accordingly instructed his scribe Brógán to note down the stories that the warriors related.

Let us take one more incident from the "Colloquy" to illustrate the ancient author's conception of Patrick's tastes and methods. One day, the story says, Caoilte was in the presence of the King of Ulster and there came to him a scholar in a beautiful green cloak with a silver brooch and a yellow shirt and a satin vest, who bore a harp and said that he was Cas Corach, the musician, and had come to get stories of the Fenians in order that he might make poems about them. The two came into Patrick's presence, and when the Apostle heard who Cas Corach was, he asked him to recite and make music.

Cas Corach took his harp and he played such splendid music for Patrick as never he had played for anyone; and to the ears of the clerics who were with Patrick it seemed to be the music of the liturgy and of hymns, praising the King of Earth and Heaven, so that they were utterly enchanted. Then the musician asked his payment from Patrick.

"What payment do you demand?" the saint inquired.

"Heaven for myself," replied Cas Corach, "for there is nought better; and that my art of music shall be lucky, and all musicians too, after me forever."

"Heaven you shall have," Patrick declared, and he promised that the art of music would be honoured forever in Ireland.

"Whatever stiffness there may be before any man of your trade, it shall go when he plays music and tell stories, and I pray that kings shall love your art, and that they shall have luck and happiness as long as they foster it without grudging."

Brógán, the scribe, praised Cas Corach's music. "It was a rare treat," said he.

"So it was," said Patrick, "only that there was just a dash of the fairies in it; and but for that, it would be the nearest thing on earth to the harmonies of heaven."

"If there is music in heaven," said Brógán, "why wouldn't there be on earth, too? So let music and musicians flourish forever."

"I do not gainsay that," said Patrick, "only just that there should not be too much of it."

All this is fabulous enough, but it shows the belief of olden authors that Patrick was favourable to the native, poetic lore. It is certain that the monks of Ireland in the following centuries of Gaelic freedom were great cherishers of the native literature. The heroic pagan tales which came down from the La Tène age, before the Christian era, would have perished from human memory a thousand years ago, but that they were written down in monasteries; the Annals were compiled in the monasteries; and in the monasteries, again, the earliest glories of Gaelic poetry were achieved. The friendliness of olden Ireland between the Church and the poetic and patriotic racial vision goes back beyond the monks of the sixth and later centuries to Patrick in the fifth, if the author of the *Colloquy* may be credited in this matter—and we think that he may. A leaning to the Gaelic legendary lore would help to explain the supercilious attitude of the Gallic Latinists to Patrick, *rusticissimus.*

It would help to explain also the rapid success of the mission.

Let us remember that the heroic legends of the Fianna and of the Kings were to the Irish people, as long as they were Gaelic in tongue and heart, just what the northern sagas are to the Germanic people; that is, an imaginative world in which dear racial memories live. They displayed the Natural virtues, and the lawful delight of man in his natural heritage. The Fenian who was so generous, so truthful, so brave, was the ideal gentleman of an open-air people. After the *Colloquy* a large cycle of poems was composed in which Oisin, the Fenian poet, was supposed to return from the Land of Youth to meet Patrick and to contend with him in long arguments, which are a sort of dramatisation of the natural and the supernatural virtues; in the end, the pagan accepts baptism, and the saint acknowledges the nobility of his dead comrades' lives before the coming of the faith.

For centuries, this literary coupling of the saint and the Fenian, of Oisin and Patrick, held a classic rank in the imagination of Ireland; and in it we discern this great truth—that in Ireland there was a reconciliation, a harmonising, between the enthusiasm of the poets and the devotion of the religious. While the northern sagas have been pitted against Christianity by some Germanic neopagans, the Irish hero-tales were given their just place as images of natural virtue, were preserved by monks, and became aids, as it were, to the higher and supernatural development of the nation. We are led by the Gaelic writers to conceive Patrick as a man who could relish a tale of the hunt or of a gallant battle, as he talked with the men whom he sought to convert to the faith—and we can believe that such a man well might succeed as we know that Patrick succeeded, and as his Irish successors succeeded when they evangelised Pictland, Northumbria, and pagan Central Europe.

3. Folklore

Innumerable are the folk-tales about Patrick. There are few parts of Ireland in which there is not some townland of which the neighbours humorously tell that St. Patrick's goat was stolen, as he went that way, and the people have been a queer lot ever since. Such was the friendly familiarity of the people with their Apostle that they used him thus in their jests. More of the tales, however, are beautiful.

In Clare, for example, it is told that when Patrick was in those parts, he chanced at some old site to come on a lump of blackened metal. It was a nugget of gold, though he did not so recognise it. He showed it to a tin-smith, asking what it was, and the tinker threw it among his old cans saying:

"It's not worth your carrying away with you."

"All the same," said Patrick, "I'll take it along, in case I find use for it"—and he did so.

When he had gone a little farther, Patrick came to a smithy, and he showed the lump of metal to the smith and asked his opinion in turn. The blacksmith weighed the lump in his hand and looked at it closely and he said: "Keep that, Sir. It is valuable enough to buy a slave's freedom."

Patrick was delighted, not so much by the gold as by the smith's honesty, and he said:

"Ever after this, the tinkers will be going from house to house to seek business, but people will come to the houses of the smiths to bring them work."

We now return from the shadow-world of legend to that of historic fact; from the doings of Pádraig mac Calpuirn, as the poets remembered him, to the latter years of Patricius, the Bishop of Armagh.

CHAPTER XII

The Saint and the Tyrant

1. To Coroticus

Out of the dimness of the Apostle's last years, a certain incident flames forth. It happened not earlier than the year 452, but it may have been at any time in the remaining nine years of life, either while he was still Metropolitan and in ceremonies of group baptisms, or when he had retired.

At some place near the coast, there had been a large baptism of neophytes. Raiders from Britain swept down upon the Irish shore, slaughtered many of the assembled Christians and carried others away captive, along with much plunder. If the affair happened in the years of Patrick's retirement, and in the neighbourhood of Saul, we can understand the statement in his Confession that even in his last days he lived in peril of a violent end. At any rate, Patrick was not far distant from the scene of the outrage, wherever it was upon the Irish coast, and at whatever time. The indignant Bishop sent a deputation of clergy with a letter to the leader of the raiders, demanding that the baptised captives be released and at least some of the booty returned. The messengers were mocked and sent away empty-handed.

Then did the Bishop, wrathful and anguished, write the document which is preserved as the *Epistle to Coroticus*. This was an open letter to the Prince of that part of Wales from which the raid had come. He described Coroticus, in Welsh Ceredig, who gave his name to Cardigan, as a *tyrannus*, signifying a chieftain of native stock who had seized power in the falling Roman realm and ruled by the strong hand, without Imperial authority. Coroticus was one of those sons of Cunedda who, with their father, came down from the north to carve out dominions for themselves in Wales when the Roman power was withdrawn. He was thus a Briton, a Celt of the same nationality and native tongue as Patrick himself, and a Christian. What infuriated Patrick most in the horrible deed committed by the soldiers of Coroticus was that it was done by Christians against Christians.

Let us hear his own words: "I, Patricius, a sinner and no doubt unlearned; I acknowledge that I have been established Bishop in Ireland. Assuredly I believe that I have received from God to be that which I am. So do I dwell in the midst of barbarous heathen, a stranger and exile for God's Love, and He is the witness if this is."

Observe the irony with which Patrick humbles himself before the British raider and describes his outraged converts as barbarous heathen. He is compelled to write, he says, because he is "moved by zeal for God and for the truth of Christ; by love for those nearest to him, and his sons for whom he gave up his fatherland and his own people and even his life unto death. "With my own hand I have written," Patrick says, "these words, to be sent to the soldiers of Coroticus—I do not say to my fellow citizens or to the fellow citizens of the Christian Romans, but to fellow citizens of the demons, by reason of their evil works. In the guise of enemies they are dead while they live, as though wishing to satiate themselves with the blood of Christian innocents, whom I in countless numbers begot unto God, and have confirmed in Christ."

Then he describes the outrage:

> On the day after that on which the newly baptised
> ones in white garments were anointed with the chrism
> which still was gleaming on their brows while they
> were cruelly cut down and slaughtered by the serfs of
> the above mentioned persons, on that day I sent a letter
> by a holy priest whom I taught from his youth, with
> other clerics, to ask that some of the plunder should
> be restored or the baptised captives. They jeered at my
> messengers. Therefore I know not which I should more
> lament, whether those who are slain or those whom
> they took captive, or those whom the devil grievously
> ensnared. In everlasting punishment they will become
> slaves of hell along with the devil; for he who commits
> sin is a slave and is called the devil's son.
>
> On this account let every man who fears God know
> that they are aliens from me and from Christ my God
> whose ambassador I am: they are patricides, they are
> fratricides, they are ravening wolves devouring the peo-
> ple of God like bread-stuff. As it is said: *The ungodly, oh
> Lord, have destroyed Thy law*—that law which in these
> last times has been so well and gently planted in Ireland
> and built up by the favour of God.

Here St. Patrick calls to mind that mysterious extension of the
Church into Ireland of which, when the outer world was falling, he
had been the instrument.

The purpose of the raiders from Wales was to sell their captives as slaves to the Scots and the Picts who lived in the North of

Britain. Patrick fastens the blame on Coroticus the Prince himself. "What shall I do, O Lord? I am exceedingly despised. Behold, around me are Thy sheep torn to pieces and despoiled by these robbers, whom Coroticus with a hostile mind has commanded. Far from the love of God is the betrayer of Christians into the hands of the Scots and Picts. Ravening wolves have swallowed up the flock of the Lord which was glowing up excellently in Ireland under the greatest care. The sons of the Gaels and the daughters of Kings who were becoming monks and virgins of Christ I am unable to number"—a proud reminder of the triumph of the Bishop's life-work. "Who among Christians would not shrink from companionship or festivity with such men?" St. Patrick goes on as he thinks of the raiders. "They have filled their houses with plunder from dead Christians; they live by rapine. They work out their punishment in eternal death."

Addressing Coroticus in the height of his anger, Patrick continues: "It is the custom of the Romans of Gaul, the Christians, to send holy and fit men to the Franks and other heathen with money to ransom baptised captives. You slay as many and sell your prisoners to a strange nation that knows not God. You deliver the members of Christ as it were to a house of ill-fame. What manner of hope in God have you, or any who co-operate with you? God will judge."

Again he continues:

> I know not what I should say or what I should speak further about the departed ones of the Son of God whom the sword has touched sharply above measure. For it is written: *Weep with them that weep*, and again, *If one member suffer let all the members suffer with it.*

Wherefore the Church bewails and will lament her sons and daughters whom the sword has not as yet slain, but who are banished and carried off to distant lands, where sin in the sight of day weighs heavy and shamefully abounds. There freemen are put up for sale, Christians are reduced to slavery, and, worst of all, to the most wicked, most vile and apostate Picts.

Therefore with sadness and grief shall I cry aloud: Oh, most lovely and loving brethren and sons whom I begot in Christ (I cannot tell the number), what shall I do for you? I am not worthy to come to the aid of either God or man. The wickedness of the wicked has prevailed against us. We are become as it were strangers.

Patrick identified himself with his Irish flock as he continues: "Perchance they do not believe that we received the one baptism or that we have one God and Father. They think it a shameful thing that we were born in Ireland." His anguish grows: "Therefore I grieve for you, I grieve, O ye most dear ones to me; yet within myself I rejoice. I have not laboured for nothing, and my journey to a strange land was not in vain. And yet, there has come to pass this crime so horrid and unspeakable. Thanks be to God, it was as baptised believers that you departed from the world to Paradise. I can behold you. You have set forth to that place where there shall be no night, nor sorrow, nor death any more, and you shall tread down the wicked and they shall be ashes under your feet. Therefore you shall reign with apostles and prophets and martyrs. You shall take everlasting Kingdoms."

Such is Patrick's consolation in his grief, that his new baptised converts have gone straight to heaven. "Aye, and where shall

Coroticus with his most villainous followers, rebels against Christ, where shall they see themselves, who distribute baptised damsels as rewards, and that for the sake of miserable temporal things which verily pass away in a moment like a cloud or smoke which is dispersed by the wind? So shall the treacherous wrong-doers perish at the presence of the Lord, but let the righteous feast in great constancy with Christ."

Finally Patrick demands the excommunication of Coroticus. The letter is to be carried to his country and read in the presence of all the people, even in the presence of the tyrant himself. The Bishop hopes that God yet may inspire those who hear to amend their lives and repent of their murderous doings: "That they may liberate the baptised captive women whom they have taken, so that they may deserve to live to God and be made whole here and in Eternity."

2. THE FRIEND OF THE SLAVES

How this remarkable letter was received, no one knows. Was Coroticus stricken in conscience by the burning words, or was he constrained by the indignation that the letter roused to do as Patrick asked? Were the unhappy Christian captives released? We cannot tell; but the indignation and intrepidity of the Bishop's language enable us to realise how he asserted his moral supremacy wherever he went during his lifetime of labour and conflict. It is evident, too, that he felt for slaves as one who had been a slave. Indeed, he said so himself. "Did I come to Ireland without God? Who compelled me to see my own folk no more? Is it from me that I show a holy compassion towards that nation which once took me captive and harried the men-servants and maidservants of my father's house?" He recalls his favoured rank. "I was born a freeman according to the flesh. I am born of a father who was a decurion; but I blush not to say nor do I regret, that I gave up my rank for the profit of others. In short, I am a slave in Christ to a strange nation on account of the unspeakable glory of the Eternal Life which is in Christ Jesus our Lord. And if my own know me not, a Prophet hath no honour in his own country."

The incident and the letter enable us to judge how Patrick the Bishop strove against the institution of slavery in the island that he made Christian. On this matter, Dr. Eoin MacNeill writes:

> Apart from the event itself, this Epistle must be understood to tell us something of the nature and effect of St. Patrick's teaching in Ireland both as regards slavery and as regards making war and dealing death upon fellow Christians. If Patrick in this manner denounced a prince of his own countrymen for the slaying and enslavement of Christians, it is not to be believed that he shrank from teaching the same doctrine to those sons of kings whom he claims to have converted and who accompanied and protected him in his journeys through Ireland.
>
> There is no doubt that under the influence of his teaching and the teaching of the Church, although here and there men and women may have been held in slavery, as in many other ways the Christian moral law was disobeyed, nevertheless slavery as a social institution soon ceased to exist, and in the seventh century, when the laws of Ireland began to be written, they take no cog-

nisance of legal slavery. We recall the juristic tradition…
in which the Druid Matha is represented foretelling to
Laoghaire the changes which Patrick was to bring about:
"He shall free the slaves."[1]

---

1.   Eoin MacNeill, *St. Patrick*.

CHAPTER XIII

Retirement

1. The Great Church

In the year 457, when he was about seventy-two years old, the mighty missionary and Metropolitan retired from his labours; but before he took up his quiet abode at Saul, there was one big undertaking to accomplish at Armagh.

We saw how he founded *Fertae Martyrum*, the Church of the Relics, in the low ground, a dozen years earlier, when his See was dignified by Rome's high favour. At that time, the lord of that country, Dáire, refused the site on the hill-top, called Willow Ridge, which the Bishop coveted. At some time after the foundation of *Na Ferta*, Patrick secured the hill-site in a curious manner.

The story says that Dáire grudgingly grazed his horses in the meadow around the church. Patrick was angry and said: "You have done ill to send your horses to disturb the little field that you gave to God." Dáire persisted in the trespass. The horses thereupon died in the churchyard field. Did they eat poisonous yew-leaves, perhaps? Angry in turn at the loss of his beasts, Dáire gave orders to his people to attack the Bishop, but a deadly sickness seized himself. Dáire's wife warned him that his misfortunes had been brought upon him by his injustice to Patrick; she forbade his people to fulfil his malicious order, and herself sent servants to ask for holy water, while concealing the reason for the request.

"But for this worthy woman," Patrick said, "Dáire would fare ill hereafter."

He sent the holy water; and Dáire, being sprinkled with it, recovered.

Sobered, the chieftain went down to *Fertae Martyrum*, bearing a precious, foreign brazen cauldron as a peace-offering.

"*Gratias agam*," Patrick said, as he accepted the gift. The phrase was one of his habitual sayings. Evidently the Latin came to his lips, much as *Go raibh maith agat* comes to the lips of Irish folk nowadays, without the reflexion that it is strange to the hearer, and so Patrick said, "I thank you" in a tongue strange to the donor. Dáire did not understand the Latin, and he grumbled on his way home. "Nothing but *gratzacham* for my fine cauldron!" Like the inconstant fellow that he was, he changed his mind again and sent servants to bring back the gift.

When the messengers told Patrick that they were to take the cauldron away, he used his customary word of courtesy, and handed the present back.

"What did the Christian say to you when you demanded the pot?" Dáire asked, on the servant's return; for evidently he was hatching over the matter.

"He only said *gratzacham*," they answered.

"What!—*gratzacham* when it is given and *gratzacham* when it is taken away?" Dáire exclaimed. "That is a strange word; there must be virtue in it. Ach! bring him back his cauldron."

This time the chieftain went with the servants himself, and the great brazen cauldron was presented to the Bishop once again. "You are a man of constancy and courage," Dáire said. "See now, I will give you also that piece of land on Willow Ridge that you asked for that other time. It is yours; go and live there."

That was how the patience and persistence of the Bishop secured for him Macha's Height—Ard-Macha, Armagh—the green hill girdled with deserted ramparts.

"Then the two set out together, viz., Patrick and Dáire, to view that wonderful offering and most gratifying gift"—so the ancient historian tells—"and together they went up the hill. On the summit they found a doe with her fawn lying on the spot where now stands the left-hand chapel in Armagh; and Patrick's people wished to seize the doe and her fawn."

This was written in the age after Patrick when the cathedral that he founded was standing, where now the Protestant cathedral stands. Patrick would not allow the doe and fawn to be slain, but "he himself took the fawn and carried it on his own shoulders, and the doe followed him tamely and confidently, just as a ewe follows the shepherd when he carries her lamb, until he loosed the fawn in a brake to the north of Armagh, where even up to our own time there are not wanting marvellous signs."

Where the doe and fawn were found, the "Great Church," Patrick's own cathedral, was founded. The brake where he loosed the fawn is said to have been on that other hill, where the present Catholic cathedral raises its twin spires towards heaven.

In what year this idyllic thing happened, we cannot tell, but the subsequent founding of the Great Church appears from the Annalists to have taken place in 457; and the Tripartite Life tells how Patrick with Dáire and the nobles of that region of Orior (as the map still calls it) ascended the hill one day "to mark it out and bless it and consecrate it." The Bishop, accompanied by his household clergy and "Ireland's Elders," proceeded to pace and measure the site, bearing the Staff of Jesus in his hand as he walked. He stepped seven-score paces to measure the diameter, or perhaps the radius, of the circular rath in which the church was to be built, with "twenty-seven paces in the great house and seventeen paces in the kitchen and seven paces in the oratory; for in that way he used to found his convents or cloisters always."

This was the last great public act of Patrick's ministry. There is reason to think that his "Great Church," unlike other Irish churches of the time, was built of stone instead of timber. This well might be; for it was the monument that he founded, as it were, as a supreme votive offering. He loved Armagh dearly, and evidently wished to exalt its dignity. He succeeded well; for Armagh's glory grew in the age that followed. Alone of the foundations of the Patrician period it did not suffer eclipse by the great monastic cities of the following century; it retained unchallenged primacy, not only in rank, but in its sanctity and scholarship.

Five centuries later, when Brian of Munster became High-King and claimed the title of *Imperator Scotorum*, this mightiest of Irish Kings visited Armagh in his royal circuit, inspected the Patrician relics so proudly cherished, and laid gifts on the altar of the Great Church, in token of Armagh's indisputable primacy. Eleven years later, having fallen in that battle which liberated Ireland from the Scandinavian yoke, Brian was borne hither to be entombed; and the approximate place where he was laid still is marked on the hill that Patrick chose and sanctified. In succeeding years of Irish freedom, the reforming Synods confirmed Armagh's primacy and recognised its colleges as the national Irish University. Never did the nation cease to venerate that Northern See, for the sake of him whose spirit seems still to abide in its holy quietude.

2. Lough Derg

Tradition says that Patrick, at some time not specified, retired to an island in the little lake in South Donegal that we call Lough Derg, to make a solitary retreat, and that there he received divine communications, as on that other retreat on the summit of the Reek in the West.[1]

Today, the pilgrimage to what we know as St. Patrick's Purgatory, at Lough Derg, is world famous. It is practised, in the immemorial traditional manner, by many hundreds of devout folk, every year, during a season which lasts from the beginning of June to the Feast of the Assumption. This pilgrimage undoubtedly is the most vivid manifestation of Irish traditional ways extant. To Pettigo, on the winding banks of Erne, train-loads of pilgrims come, and then some miles of sour, brown heath are to be traversed by a road which was marked by wayside crosses until bigots destroyed them in the last century. Men of all nations, princes of mediaeval Europe, famous churchmen of the ages, have gone barefoot along that rising road, into the peaty wilderness where suddenly the broad lough is revealed, with a few small islands on its bosom. Boats rowed by huge oars that need several boatmen to pull them—just such boats as must have been used in olden days—ferry the fasting pilgrims to one island, where ancient stone crosses mark the stations of the pilgrimages, and hostels for men and for women stand on either side of a majestic basilica.

---

1.   Shane Leslie, *Saint Patrick's Purgatory: A Record from History and Litera-*
     ture. This monumental volume contains the principle documents, native
     and foreign, which relate to the Purgatory, with maps, notes, and other
     apparatus.

It is a sublime spot—austere as the world's end, beaten upon by the oceanic storms, drenched for half the year in storm clouds that foam over the hills, and again illuminated by magnificent skies. The country around is fit only for sheep, and homesteads are little white specks here and there in the wild expanse.

For three days, living on a little dry bread and black tea, the barefoot pilgrims watch and pray—one night there is vigil in the church—and cycles of devotions are observed at the age-worn crosses of Patrick, Brigid, and Catherine. The bodily rigour is unequalled on any other European pilgrimage; and we dare say that the spiritual exaltation on that little island amid grey waters and peatclad, empty hills, is not excelled. Here the old, old race is conspicuous; for the pilgrimage is specially dear to the folk who were in Donegal when Patrick was there, long, long ago. No stranger has made the pilgrimage without discovering, among many other things, the inner life of the Gael.

There are no records of the pilgrimage going back farther than the twelfth century, when the Anglo-Norman invaders began to frequent Lough Derg and one of them, a knight named Owen, according to a remarkable Cistercian book, saw a vision of Purgatory within an island cave, supposed to be that in which Patrick had prayed. The mediaeval fame of the pilgrimage is owing chiefly to the story of Knight Owen; this, and certain other visionary stories from Ireland are held to have given Dante his creative inspiration. Nevertheless, it is certain that the pilgrimage goes back further than the Norman vogue; for we find the Gaelic poets, most conservative of minds and most reluctant to be moved by foreign influence, making the pilgrimage and writing of it. The greatest of Gaelic religious poets, Donnchadh Mór O Dálaigh, Abbot of Boyle (thirteenth century), has a poem in which he laments the hardness of his heart, his slowness to tears, at Lough Derg.

> *Truagh mo thuras ar Loch Dearg*
> *A righ na gceall is na gclog:*

"Alas for my pilgrimage to Lough Derg, O King of the churches and the bells; I have come to weep Thy bruises and Thy wounds, yet not a tear comes from my eyes." In later times, a company of the chief Gaelic poets makes the pilgrimage, and all compose poems on "the fair Rome of the Western World"—"Lough Derg is Eire's chief Rome."[2] Mark the use of *Rome* as a noun signifying *sanctuary*. It is curiously fitting to Lough Derg today; for now the new church on Station Island bears the rank of a Minor basilica, an honour conferred on it by Pope Pius XI in 1930. The Papal Arms are over the great door.

This strong-rooted and essentially Irish pilgrimage could not have risen after the Invasion. It is true that the island traditionally visited by Patrick is not Station Island but Saints' Island, near by; but Station Island has been the scene of the devotions ever since an ancient religious house was built there, to leave the crosses which now serve the pilgrims' needs.

We are persuaded, therefore, that the story of Patrick's retreat to Lough Derg, coming to us through so pure a traditional channel, is no fiction. It accords with his known custom to choose solitary places for contemplation and prayer, as when he went out on Slemish as a slave-boy and climbed the Reek as a Bishop. The neglect of his early biographers to record the retreat, and the survival of

---

2.   *Poems of Tadhg Dall Ó Huiginn*, edited by E. Knott.

the tradition among the people, may have this simple explanation: that Patrick went to the lough when he had laid down his Primatial office. He made the famous Lenten retreat on the Reek when the first stage of his work was complete and he was about to seek Rome's approbation. What more likely than that the occasion of his retreat to Lough Derg should be his laying down of office, when his life-work was complete?

So we imagine him, when he had founded the "Great Church" at Armagh and had surrendered authority to his chosen successor, Benignus, going to the island solitude, in the first year of his retirement, perhaps in the Lent of 458. The mystic knew how to draw close to God in silent places; and there he would render his account in prayer and devote himself, as pilgrims still must do, to the supreme concern of his life, his own salvation. His work had succeeded; he was conscious of that, as we learn soon afterwards from his Confession. Yet he bared his soul to his conscience, and sought to see his record with the searching eyes of divine justice. We know also from his Confession that he was diffident, humble, hopeful, still striving, still persevering, still conscious that he was a sinner. *Ego Patricius peccator* he called himself. What he said to God, and what sublime consolation he received, are the secrets that even tradition does not tell; but, on an immeasurably humbler scale every pilgrim soul at the Purgatory repeats that mystical intercourse.

If we are right, then, in assuming that Patrick's retreat at Lough Derg was made in the years of his retirement, when his acts, so to speak, were those of a private person, we have a ready explanation, as has been said, of his early biographers' silence on this matter. This retreat was no part of the public career of the Apostle. On the other hand, it would be remembered locally, especially at the monastery which Patrick's friend St. Dabheoc established at the lough, and a local devotion would follow, which would become rooted, as it were, in the very life of the Donegal people. Have we not met old Donegal men who have walked across the mountains to Lough Derg, summer after summer, for fifty consecutive years? From a local devotion, that pilgrimage would grow, after centuries, with the devotion to Patrick himself, which also grew, as we know well. Thus a most sacred moment in the private and interior life of the saint would become, as it has become, a centre of inspiration to the faithful; and generations that inherit that holy Catholic life which Patrick brought to Ireland, share also his mystical nearness to God.

CHAPTER XIV

Confessions Before Death

The outpouring of the great heart of our own St. Patrick... Like the Epistles of St. Paul, it proves its own authorship; so that the most sceptical critic cannot doubt its authenticity, for he is silenced when he reads it.

Archbishop Healy, *Life and Writings of St. Patrick*

There is no more affecting document in any literature than the Confession *of St. Patrick.*

Dr. Helena Concannon, *Saint Patrick*

The wonderful Apologia *which has come down to us from his own pen;...judged as the self-revelation of a personal spiritual experience, only the Apocalypse excels it in sublimity.*

Dr. R. A. Stewart Macalister, *Ancient Ireland*

1. Last Days

Mountains of Mourne rise from the golden strand of Iveagh and Lecale to peaks that shimmer in the misty sky, Donard and Bernagh are steep and bare, and the cloud shadows pass over them in wave after wave of cool blue; the lesser hills are hidden in pine forest, with mysterious black depths. All the foreground is golden whin and white hawthorn, mass upon mass of clustered brilliance, with narrow grey roads winding to lime-walled homesteads. The sea wind sounds in the young greenery; the lark's song and the robin's make sweet harmony against the deeper, distant cawing of some rookery. A countryman drives home his sleek, black cattle from the crisp pastures, and the voices of children at play tell where his home is hidden behind the hill. He pauses with evident respect to receive a kindly word from a certain grey, spare cleric, who is walking in the cool of the evening to the eminence which commands the lough and its multitudinous little isles.

What peace there is in this country of Lecale, between the mountains and the blue, blue seal. The aged churchman who is taking his evening walk is in the right country (you would say) to commune with heaven. His mystical soul is surely overflowing with a happiness that matches all the loveliness of Mourne. For one, two, three, almost four years, he has been dwelling here in retirement, greatly loved by the country-folk for his simplicity. "Ooh, sure the Bishop's just like one of ourselves," they say, when he has passed a few words with them, advising them in a knowledgeable way about their beasts and saying "God speed the plough!" Aye, Mourne seems as beautiful and as tranquil as the heaven that is shining already in the old Bishop's soul, but think through what great tribulation he came into this peace. This austere, gentle, furrowed, white-haired churchman, aged about seventy-five, is Patricius the Bishop, who has wrought such a work as no other apostle since the first ever accomplished. He has taken a world beyond the Roman world for Christ, carrying the frontiers of the Church to the end of the known world, and has won to the faith a vigorous, teeming, ancient nation which will send forth, in the following centuries, a thousand and ten thousand apostolic souls like his own, to work like his, those sons of whom he spoke—*filii quos in Christo genui, enumerare nequeo,* sons whom he begot in Christ, and could not number.

Sad and strange to tell, even in those last years of the Bishop's life, when all should be quiet as a cloister, there were dangers still about him, and, what hurt him more, jealous folk in Ireland and in Britain and in Gaul criticised his work cruelly and pursued him with unjust charges. He was accused of self-seeking, and his homely, racy personality was ridiculed as rustic. Like most lonely men, he was intensely sensitive, and his last days were tortured by the criticisms which, as he feared, must weaken his influence and endanger that work which he had built with so much love and pain. These things we learn from his apologia, his *Confession Before Death,* as he described the statement which he wrote at this time.

In the year 457, as we saw, he gave up his great charge at Armagh, the headship of the Church that he had established in Ireland, to that disciple whom he had named Benignus—the boy, the chief's son, who had laid flowers in the weary missionary's bosom when he slept after landing on the Irish shore; Benignus, who carried the books when the little company marched from Slane to take Tara from the Druids. The story tells how Benignus, obedient and full of faith, endured the trial of fire to which the Druids challenged the Christian witnesses.

Once when the great Bishop turned from his vexatious labours among the kings and the people to pray in a solitary place beneath the stars, having with him young Benignus, the "dear and trusty boy," he tested this disciple with a question.

"My son, tell me, if you can, if you behold what I behold?"

The chief's son said: "I know the things that you see; I behold the heavens open, and the Son of God and His angels."

"Worthy are you," the Bishop said, "to be my successor."

From 457 to the Lent of 461, Patrick had lived in that remote part of the North, Lecale, which he loved because he had begun his mission there, and doubtless preferred for his last years because it was far from busy places like Armagh or Dunshaughlin, near Tara, where his second-in-command of the mission, Secundinus, had died ten years before. In the second year of his retirement, Patrick heard of the death of Auxilius, so that only one of his three great Gallic helpers, Iserninus, still lived on, away down at Rathvilly, among the Leinstermen. Perhaps he likened himself to "Oisin after the Fianna," in the proverbial saying that he knew from those Fenian stories which he liked to hear from old soldiers who were among his converts.

Though he had given himself to Ireland, he never forgot the unity of the Christian world—great Augustine's City of God—but Augustine, and the other mighty churchmen whose names had rung in the world when he was a monk at Lérins and Auxerre, all had passed away. St. Jerome, translator of the Scriptures, was dead. St. John Chrysostom, "the Golden-Tongued," the Patriarch of Constantinople who had held Christendom together though the Empire split, and St. Cyril of Alexandria, who championed the Mother of God, *Theotokos*, had passed into history. The Gallic St. Germanus, who had won Pope St. Celestine's approval of the Irish mission, had died a few years after Armagh was founded. Only Pope Leo the Great, whom we revere as St. Leo I, who had approved and confirmed Patrick at his ever memorable visit to Rome, still lived, and was to outlive the Apostle of Ireland by a few weeks.

As for the secular state of the world, it was changed beyond all likeness to what the boy Patricius had known. The Goths had become masters of South Gaul and the Visigothic Kingdom of Spain was rising; the Vandals were masters of Augustine's Africa, and Italy was controlled by one Recimir, commander of Barbarian mercenaries. Only a few years earlier—about the time when Patrick was being honoured by the convert King of Cashel—the Scourge of God, Attila the Hun, had shaken what remained of the Roman world; in 452, the Huns had been turned back, not by Roman arms, but by the spiritual strength of Pope Leo, who faced them and rebuked them and dominated them in the manner of the intrepid Patrick at Tara. The Roman world had broken down, but the Church, in such souls as Leo and Patrick, was beginning to mould a new world out of the Barbarians, who feared no arms but were awed by the spirit of Christ.

Aye, Leo on the Continent, and Patrick in the ultimate island-kingdom, had laid the foundation of the Christendom which was to rise from the ruins of the empire. Henceforth, *Roman* would signify something new. *Ecclesia Scotorum, immo Romanorum, ut Christiani ita et Romani sitis*—the Book of Armagh records these words of Patrick, in his instruction that the *Kyrie, Eleison* should be sung in the Irish churches: "Church of the Irish, nay of the Romans, as you are Christians so be ye Romans."

Amid so much change, for better and worse, an old man longed to be with some old friends, who had known the world that was gone. The lonely missionary Bishop at Saul often desired strongly to visit Gaul and meet the survivors of his brethren. We learn this, too, from his Confession.

2. "I, Patrick, a Sinner"

He took up his pen and wrote, addressing in the one document his critics and his friends, the churchmen of Gaul and his converts of

Ireland. *"Ego Patricius peccator, rusticissimus et minimus omnium fidelium…"* So he began the Confession, written in his last days on earth.[1]

> I am Patrick, a sinner, the most backward and the least
> of all the Faithful, and held by many in contempt. I had
> for my father Calpornius, a deacon, the son of Potitus,
> a presbyter; who belonged to the village of Bannavem
> Taberniae. Near by he had a little country house, where
> I was taken prisoner. At that time I was barely sixteen
> years of age.

Thus does Patrick plunge into his story, with no waste of words. "I knew not the true God," he continued, as he recalls his careless boyhood, "and I was led into captivity in Ireland with many thousand persons, as we deserved; for we turned away from God and kept not His commandments, and we were not obedient to our priests, who used to admonish us concerning our salvation. And the Lord brought upon us the indignation of His wrath, and scattered us among many nations even to the uttermost part of the earth, where now my littleness may be seen among strangers."

That is all that the old Bishop tells of his youth in the Roman world before he was carried prisoner to the land that the Romans never had subdued. "And there the Lord opened the understanding of my unbelief, so that (though tardily) I might recall to mind my sins and be converted with all my heart to the Lord my God, who hath regarded my humility…." Mark how Patrick, whose language

---

1.   For our extracts from the *Confession,* here and elsewhere, we have used
     Archbishop Healy's translation, with some modification.

teems with phrases from the Scriptures, borrows from our Lady the words that he uses here: *Respexit humilitatem meam*. He breaks into his own *Magnificat*, a splendid burst of praise. "I cannot conceal, nor is it indeed fitting, the great favours and the great grace which the Lord has deigned to bestow upon me in the land of my captivity; for this is the return we make, that after our chastening and after our recognition of God, we should exalt and proclaim His wondrous works before every nation which is under heaven; for there is no other God." And here his praise swells into a majestic adoration of the Trinity:

> For there is no other God, nor ever was, nor ever will there be hereafter, save God the Father unbegotten, without beginning, from whom is all beginning, upholding all things, as we say; and His Son Jesus Christ, whom we likewise testify to have been always with the Father before the world's beginning, spiritually and ineffably with the Father, begotten before all beginning.
>
> And by Him were made all things visible and invisible, who was made man and having triumphed over death was taken up to the Father in heaven; and to Him the Father gave all power above every name, so that in the name of Jesus every knee should bow of those that are in heaven, on earth, and under the earth, and every tongue should confess to Him that Jesus Christ is the Lord and God in whom we believe.
>
> And we expect His coming soon to take place, the Judge of the living and the dead, who will render to every one according to his works.

And He has poured out on us abundantly the Holy
Ghost, the gift and pledge of immortality, who maketh
those who believe and obey to become children of God
and joint-heirs with Christ, whom we confess and adore
as one God in the Trinity of the Sacred Name.

Such is the keynote of Patrick's mind and devotion.

3. REBUKE TO THE LITERATI!

"Yet, though in many things I am imperfect, I wish my brethren
and kinsfolk to know the kind of me," the aged Bishop says, as he
resumes his story, "so that they may understand my soul's desire.
For a long time I have thought of writing, but hitherto have hesi-
tated." He feared, he says, the criticism of those scholarly folk who
have studied classical and sacred letters with equal perfection and
are masters of style; great folk who never had to change their vernacular, as he did, but were ever perfecting their native Latin. As
for him, it were vain in his old age to seek to acquire that polish
which he failed to attain in youth, owing to his sins—meaning,
apparently, that he neglected his lessons when he was a boy in
Roman Britain. Was he not taken captive, while yet a beardless boy,
before he knew "what he ought to seek and what to avoid." He still
felt diffident, he says, not having a concise literary style—"because,
not being a scholar, I cannot express myself with brief words." Most
writers make much of Patrick's diffidence; but, as in his Letter to
Coroticus, we seem to detect a quiet irony in these tributes to the
scholarship of other people, mighty in their language, petty in their
deeds. "For," says he, "as the spirit strives, it reveals both soul and

sense." That is to say, words may mean much or little, but sincerity will find the way to make itself understood.

He, then, was uncultivated, an exile, and ignorant, like a stone that lies in deep mire; but, after his humiliation, "He that is mighty raised me and placed me on the top of the wall." (Is there not a flavour of Gaelic style in that saying?) "Wherefore, be ye filled with admiration, O ye both small and great who fear the Lord, and ye also, my lords, ye rhetoricians; and hear and consider. Who was it that exalted me, the fool, from the midst of those who seemed wise and highly skilled in letters, powerful in language and in all things beside? For me, though verily contemptible to this world, He inspired beyond others in spite of all; that with fear and reverence and without blame I should serve faithfully the strange nation to whom the love of Christ led me and dedicated me, if I should be worthy, for all my life, that in humility and truth I should serve them." He harps on the word *serve*, who was a servant first by capture and then by self-sacrifice.

Who were those rhetoricians whom he surely ironically addressed, *vos dominicati rethorici*? Some writers think that they were secular scholars from Gaul, of the rank called *rhetorician*, or as we would say nowadays, professors; scholars who had fled to Ireland from the barbarians. Others say that he was alluding to the Scholars of Gaul and Britain in their own lands. It may be that he had in mind native Irish scholars of the Gaelic tradition; for the *fili*, the poets of the druidic schools had ranks corresponding to the rhetoricians of the Classical schools in Gaul, and often were every whit as haughty. Whatever the nationality of these proud gentry, the type is unmistakable; it is the pedant, the "highbrow," who is always met in a decadent civilisation. Living in a futile world of unnatural refinement, the "highbrow" scorns the man of faith and deeds.

Patrick's diffidence has misled many writers of modern times, not familiar with the Latin of the fifth century, who have taken up his *Confessio* and found it crude as compared with the Latin of Cicero or Livy. The truth is that his diction was as good as that of most authors of that age, short of masters such as St. Jerome or St. Augustine; he was ignorant only in the eyes of the high-flown literary schools that flourished in that age of decay as they do in our own. Authors, like those who wrote the elegant nothings of the *Hisperica Famine*, had intimidated the reading public of the fifth century as the decadents of the literary reviews intimidate fools today. Patrick's apologies to the pedants must be read as a rebuke to folly and as the indignation of the honest mind. He wrote for a purpose more serious than that of the literary caste. "Even if I had the gift of fine language," he says, "I would not be silent," and adds: "for my duty's sake." That is to say, he is required by God's will to show forth the work of God in his soul, and, lettered or unlettered, he will do it. If he is criticised adversely, he recalls that it is written: *The stammering tongue shall quickly learn to speak peace*; and how much more should we wish to do so, of whom it is said that we ourselves are *the epistle of Christ for salvation unto the ends of the earth*. His message may not be eloquent, but it is powerful and effective; for it is written in hearts, "not with ink, but by the Spirit of the Living God."

He adds a curious saying. "And again the Spirit witnesseth, *Rusticity, too, was ordained by the Most High*." Remember that Patrick's mission was to a rural nation; that he carried the faith from Roman cities to the Irish countryside, being "the first monk missioner formed by the new rural Christianity." To the critics of his mission and of his language, of his life and of his manners, the city folk of the Roman world, he says: "Rusticity is God's work, too." Admire the quiet irony of this irascible saint.

4. His Own Account

"And neither was I worthy," the old man goes on, resuming his argument, "nor such that the Lord should grant so much to His poor servant"; and he tells the story of his wondrous preparation and call. To Patrick, the hand of God was plain in his captivity, his release, his summons to Ireland in a vision, his long preparation in Gaul, the awful trial of his rejection, and his final adoption as bishop and mission-leader. To us, too, when we analyse the strange sequence of events, the providential direction of it all is marvellous and unmistakable. If ever divine purpose was manifest in a life, it was in that of the slave-boy of Slemish.

Mark the mystical preparation!—"Now after I came to Ireland, daily I pastured herds and often in the daytime I used to pray; more and more there grew in me the love of God and the fear of Him, and my faith was enlarged and my spirit was stirred, till I prayed in one day a hundred times and at night nearly as often, so that I used to linger in the woods and on the mountain. Before dawn, I would awake to prayer in snow and in frost and in rain, and I was none the worse for it; nor was there any sluggishness in me such as I now see, for then the Spirit burnt within me"—The old man remembers the ardour of youth's prayers. "And there it was, to wit, that on a certain night I heard in my sleep a voice saying to me: '*Thou fastest well. Soon thou art to go to thy fatherland.*'"

We have told what followed; how the boy Patrick was told in his sleep that his ship was ready, and fled, following the miraculous summons; and how he came with the ship's company into the Roman world and found a wilderness, for the barbarians had passed ravening through Gaul of the vineyards and the gilded cities. There, in the utter loneliness, he suffered a night of agony near to despair, and he cried in his sleep (though he knew not how the words came into his spirit) the very words of the dying Lord: "*Eli, Eli, lama sabachthani?*"[2] and behold, as he prayed thus, the splendour of the sun shone forth, and relief came to the starving company. Some years he spent in Gaul and Italy and in the islands of the Mediterranean, that is, in monastic Lérins of the Saints, and again he was in Britain, among his own people. Of his continental sojourn he tells nothing. The people for whom he wrote knew all about that; what he wanted to tell was the interior facts. So he passes over the outward movements of the monk Patricius, and describes the vision which came to him as he dwelt in Britain, the vision of one who bore a letter that was inscribed *The Voice of the Irish*. He heard the voices of the people of that wooded island over the Western Sea, and was "greatly touched in heart." To him, more mightily than to any other man who ever lived, came that overpowering magnetism of the love of Ireland that exiles feel and recognise in his few, simple words.

Nevertheless, he says, he did not hasten to Ireland. He suffered the terrific trial of choice and rejection for the Irish mission in 431. Of the trial to his soul, he writes in words that shake us; "Truly I was thrust at, on that day, that I might fall here and forever"; but he does not narrate the strange turn of events by which he got his heart's desire. "Towards Ireland of my own accord I made no move." *Non sponte pergebam.* Are Patrick's words an echo of the words of Aeneas, just one Classical phrase coming to his pen?

---

2.   In the Confession, this passage runs *Dum Clamarem Heliam Heliam*. It has puzzled most translators, and several represent Patrick as crying *Helios*, which makes little sense. Dr. R. A. S. Macalister, in his *Ancient Ireland* (p. 170, note), solves the riddle. Patrick woke as he cried the Biblical words *Eli, Eli*, etc.

Italiam non sponte sequor, said the founder of the Roman nation; "not of my own accord I seek out Italy." It is a higher power that moved Aeneas in fable and Patrick in fact.

So in Ireland his work was cast, and he saw the undertaking in a light that we can realise only if we recall that the great contemporaries of his youth thought of Rome's fall in 410 as the fall of the world; and Patrick had lived to see the Roman world trampled down by Gothic and Vandal hordes—the church-destroying Saxons were raging through Christian Britain even when he wrote. "God has heard me," he wrote, "so that I, though so little learned, should undertake *in these last days* this work so holy and so marvellous, that I should imitate in some measure those whom the Lord long ago foretold would proclaim His Gospel for a testimony unto all nations before the end of the world. Accordingly, as we see, this has come to pass; and behold, we are witnesses that the Gospel has been preached to the places beyond which no man dwells— *usque ubi nemo ultra est!*" Compare his Epistle to Coroticus: "It was not my own grace, but God that put this earnest care into my heart, that I should be one of the hunters or fishers whom long ago God foretold would come *in the last days.*"

Patrick almost certainly had in mind that Epistle of St. Paul in which the earlier great missionary defended himself; and we find a Pauline echo in Patrick's next words. "It were long to narrate all my toils in detail, or even in part. Briefly, I will tell in what manner God most pitiful often saved me both from servitude and from twelve perils by which my life was jeopardised, besides many ambushes and troubles which I cannot set forth in words lest I should weary those who read.

5. A Charge Answered

Next Patrick explains why he refused the gifts which were pressed upon him, during his missionary work, and thereby offended both the donors and some of his seniors; that is, the high clergy in Gaul. He was resolved that his preaching of the Gospel to the Irish people should be done without payment or reward from them; he never would surrender his independence, even though others should profit, "And if I should be worthy I am ready to give also my life freely and without hesitation for God's name, and in Ireland I desire to spend it till I die, if God will grant it. For I am greatly a debtor to God, who granted me such a grace that many peoples through me should be regenerated in God and afterwards confirmed, and that clergy should be ordained for them everywhere, as a nation newly come to faith whom God took from the ends of the earth…. And in Ireland I wish to wait for His promise, who verily never fails.

"It was highly necessary," Patrick continues, "that we should spread wide our nets so that a great multitude should be taken for God, and that everywhere there should be clergy to baptise and to exhort the poor and needy people;…and behold how Ireland, whose people never had the knowledge of God, but hitherto adored idols and unclean things: behold how they are become a people of the Lord and are called sons of God. Sons of the royal Irish and the daughters of princes—see how they have become monks and virgins of Christ."

Devout women, he says, used to present him with little gifts and to lay their ornaments upon the altar; but he returned them, even though it gave scandal to those good folk. "But I did it on account of the hope of immortality, and that I might keep myself cautiously in all matters, so that I should not give unbelievers cause in the smallest thing to defame or to detract.

"When, therefore, I baptised so many thousands, did I desire from any of them the half of a scruple? If so, tell me, and I will restore it. Or when the Lord through my poor means ordained clergy everywhere and I gave them my ministration *gratis*, did I ever ask from any so much as the price of my shoe-leather?

"Sometimes I would give presents to the kings beside the hire that I paid their people who accompanied me; and yet they seized me once with my company—and on that day they strongly wished to kill me, but my time had not come, though they robbed us of all and bound me with iron. On the fourteenth day the Lord freed me from their power and what was ours was restored to us, through God and the worthy friends whom I had provided beforehand." This is the only account we have of an affair in which some powerful personage, perhaps Conall or Laoghaire, intervened to save Patrick from a hostile pagan prince; but it is thought that he refers to the violent efforts made to prevent his entry to Tirawley, when he won Connacht for the Church.

Patrick tells, too, how lavishly he spent on the provision of guides "that you might enjoy me, and I you, in God. I do not repent of it, nor is it enough for me. Still I spend and will spend more"— he says to the Irish people—"for the Lord is powerful to repay me hereafter, that I may be spent for your souls."

6. The Virgins of Christ

Noteworthy in Patrick's life-work was his encouragement of the religious life among women. Beside such examples as those daughters of the High-King whose vocation he confirmed at the Well of Clebach, there were the many others who became workers in the mission—holy women who made vestments and performed similar offices.

"And especially," says Patrick, "there was one blessed lady, of Scotic (i.e., royal Irish) birth, noble, most beautiful, of adult age, whom I myself baptised, and after a few days she came to us for a certain purpose, confiding that she had received an intimation from God that she should become a Virgin of Christ and thereby come nearer to God. Thanks be to God, on the sixth day afterwards, well and eagerly she accomplished that purpose. Even so do also all God's virgins, not with the accord of their fathers; but they endure persecution and lying insults from their parents, and none the less their number still grows—and we know not the number of our folk who are reborn thus, beside widows and chaste livers.

"But," Patrick adds, reminding us of a bitter reality of his times—"they who are detained in slavery suffer exceedingly; they endure terror and menace. Yet the Lord has given grace to many of my handmaids, so that although forbidden they steadfastly follow the example (of the free)."

Because of the suffering of these Christians in bondage, Patrick says, he would not leave them; and therefore, though he had desired much to go to Britain to his own people, and farther, into Gaul, to see "my Lord's good folk" (his fellow monks of other days, his class fellows), yet he felt bound to remain in Ireland. "The Spirit testifieth to me that He would hold me guilty," and he feared to lose his harvest if he neglected it. "The Lord Christ commanded me that I should dwell the remainder of my days with them."

Is it not a moving thing to know that Patrick denied himself the solace of return, or a visit, to Gaul, where he would meet his dearest friends once more—denied himself chiefly for the sake of the suffering women of Ireland.

7. I Have Kept the Faith

We have noted one passage that recalls St. Paul. Like the Apostle of the Gentiles, the Apostle of the Irish had a stormy soul. He gives a glimpse of the interior warfare of his life.

Having told how he hopes to end his days among his converts, he goes on: "Now I hope this as I ought, but I do not rely on myself as long as I shall be in this body of death, for he who strives daily to turn me away from the faith and from that pure and unfeigned religion which I have set before me to keep to my life's end in Christ my Lord, is strong; and the enemy of the flesh always draws us towards death, that is, to delights whose end is misery. And I know in part in what matter I have not led a perfect life like other believers; but I confess to my Lord and am not ashamed in His sight, for I lie not, in that ever since I knew Him in my youth the love of God grew in me and the fear of Him, and unto now, by the Lord's favour, I have kept the faith."

He has not written, he says, to win honour from his readers. "There suffices that honour which is not seen but is realised in the heart"—truly the saying of a great soul. "Nevertheless, I perceive that in this world I have been exalted above measure by the Lord. I was not worthy, nor am I such that He should grant this to me; for, as I well know, poverty and calamity suit me better than riches and delights. Christ the Lord was poor for our sakes; and I, even if I should desire wealth, I have it not, and daily I look for a violent death or to be robbed or reduced to slavery or the like. Yet, on account of the promises of heaven, I fear none of these things, and I have cast myself into the hands of the omnipotent God."[3] Perhaps the raid by the soldiers of Coroticus had taken place recently, when these words were written, and Patrick so identified himself with his converts as to make their peril his own.

"Behold now," he goes on, "I commend my soul to my most faithful God, whose ambassador I am in my lowliness.... And now what shall I render to the Lord for all the things He hath rendered to me? What shall I say or promise to my Lord, since I have nothing save what He Himself has given to me; but He knoweth that fully and greatly I desire and have been ready that He should grant me to drink of His cup, as He hath granted to others who love Him."

8. A Prayer for Ireland

"Wherefore may it never happen to me from my God," Patrick prays, remembering Ireland ever, "that I should lose His people whom He hath purchased at the ends of the earth. I pray God that He may give me perseverance and deign that I may render faithful witness unto Him until my passing.

"And if ever I achieved aught of good for the sake of my God whom I love, I ask Him to grant me that I may pour out my blood together with those converts and captives for His name, even though I should lack burial or my body should be divided most miserably limb from limb for the dogs and wild beasts or that fowl

---

3. Patrick's stress on the spiritual benefits of poverty should be compared with the words of Santa Teresa on the same subject. The similarity of language is remarkable, and demonstrates an identity of spirituality.

of the air should devour it; for surely I think if this should happen to me, I have gained my soul with my body."

Surely this is written in recent memory of the outrage by Coroticus' men. Patrick wants to give his life with the victims. The hope of salvation rises to a glorious certitude, when he makes himself one with those who are newly dead after baptism. "For without any doubt we shall rise on that day with the brightness of the sun, that is in the glory of our Redeemer Christ Jesus," he writes, and he continues with that exalted passage which we quoted when we described him as a preacher.

He draws to an end. His story is told. He has been slighted, he has been accused, and this is his defence, his Confession—that, though he is all that his detractors say of him as to ignorance and slavery, yet he is a slave for a high reason, the love of God. "Behold, again and again I repeat my confession. I testify in truth and in exultation of heart before God and His holy angels that I had no purpose save the Gospel and its promise in returning to that people from whom aforetime with difficulty I escaped. But I pray those who believe and fear God, whosoever among them shall deign to look upon or receive this writing which Patrick the sinner and the ignorant wrote in Ireland, that never shall it be said that any little thing that I have done or demonstrated by God's pleasure was done out of my poor merit; but judge ye, and let it be believed, that it was *donum Dei*, God's own gift."

That is the end. "*Et haec est confessio mea antequam moriar*," the old Bishop writes. "And so *this* is my confession before I die"— and his old eyes look forth on the high mountains of Mourne, among whom his children in Christ lived and live to this day; and the old man smiles. The mystic's work in the world is done.

CHAPTER XV

Cece Sacerdos Magnus

1. The Death of Patrick

Now, after these great marvels, namely, after raising the dead to life, after healing lepers and blind and deaf and halt and sick folk of every kind besides: after ordaining bishops and priests and deacons and folk of every other grade in the Church: after teaching the men of Ireland and after baptising them: after founding churches and monasteries: after destroying idols and images and the knowledge of wizardry, the time of holy Patrick's death drew nigh.

THE TRIPARTITE LIFE

In the early Spring of the year 461, when, by our reckoning, he was aged seventy-six, and was dwelling "in the extremity of Ulster"; that is, in the remote, quiet, fair land of Lecale at kindly Saul, Patrick knew that his death was drawing near. He sent to Armagh for a company to bear him thither. Another account says, "he began to go to Armagh"; that is, he started painfully upon the road that lies to the north of long Slieve Croob to Dromore and through the orchard country to the Primatial hill beyond the Bann. He desired to end his days in the spiritual capital of Ireland. His wish has been preserved in an ancient verse:

> *Doroega port neiseirgi*
> I have chosen as my place of resurrection,
> Armagh my church,...
> It is Armagh that I love,
> Beloved town, beloved hill,
> A stronghold that my soul haunteth—
> Emania of the warriors will be waste.

Somewhere on the road through the east of Ulster, Patrick learnt that he was not to have his wish. Perhaps the ways, in a harsh winter, were too toilsome for the aged, work-worn churchman, and his strength failed. A bush by the wayside glowed with unearthly light, and the angel Victor, who had summoned him to Ireland in dream so long before, now spoke from the bush to him and said: "It is not in Armagh that your resurrection is to be. Go back to the townland that you have left, namely, Saul, the Barn; for it is there that you shall die and not in Armagh."

To this interior message, Patrick's reply is recorded: "I have no command of my freedom, it is bondage to the end."

"It has been granted to you by God," the angel said, "that your dignity and authority, your devotion and your doctrine, shall be in Armagh as if you were alive therein."

So the old writer tells, presumably preserving a tradition of what the broken old man told his friends when he came back to them at Saul, never to see Armagh again. He was attended in his last illness by St. Tassach, a veteran of the mission, who was bishop at Raholp, between Saul and the sea.

According to the poem called Fiacc's Hymn, the illness was painful; the old man did not die easily. "Patrick's soul from his body, it is with pangs they were parted." Bishop Tassach gave him the Last Sacraments and then waited with him to the end. On March 17th, in mid-Lent, "he sent forth his spirit to heaven." So passed Patricius, the Apostle of the Irish, whom the ancient Gaelic homily described as "a righteous man, verily, with purity of nature like the patriarchs; a true pilgrim, like Abraham; mild, forgiving from the heart, like Moses; a praise-giving psalmist, like David; a choice vessel for proclaiming truth, like Paul the Apostle.... A flashing fire with the fervour of the Sons of Life, inflaming charity; a lion for strength, a dove for gentleness; a serpent for prudence and cunning as to the good; kind, humble, merciful to the Sons of Life; dark and stern towards the Sons of Death; a labourious and serviceable slave to Christ."

On the first night after Patrick's death "the angels of the elements" watched his body with spiritual songs, and the odour of divine grace came from it. For twelve nights, the eminent men of Ireland watched, with hymns and psalms and canticles. No doubt the long space of twelve days between death and burial was designed to allow Patrick's fellow bishops to be summoned and to assemble from distant places. Iserninus, who survived Patrick, would have over a hundred miles to travel from Rathvilly. In that time of watching, there was no darkness in the whole region, but angelic radiance—a poetic way of saying, no doubt, that every house was illuminated, as if the wake were kept throughout the Island Plain. "And so night was not seen in the whole of that region during the days of lamentation."

Whatever lies behind the legendary or rhetorical account of the death and burial, it is plain that Patrick resembled the great men of Ireland in later days, in suffering opposition and bitter criticism in life, to be appreciated justly and lamented universally at death. The zeal to honour him in death mounted to a scandalous pitch. There was a contest between the men of Oriel and the Uí Néill on the one side, and the Ulidians of East Ulster on the other, for the privilege of burying the great Bishop in their own territory. The story speaks of conflict, verging on battle; of a miraculous flooding by the Quoile river, which separated the hosts, and of a mysterious optical illusion which caused both to think that they had secured the bier. MacNeill thinks[1] that Patrick foresaw the dispute for his remains and gave orders for a secret burial. It seems to us likelier that the clergy at Saul, when the turbulence of the rivals threatened scandal, thwarted the enthusiasts by some ruse and hurried the body away to a place of sepulture which was not disclosed. Whatever the facts behind the obscure story, the whereabouts of Patrick's grave were not known, and in this he was likened by the old Gaelic writers to Moses. A hundred years later, it is said, St. Columcille revealed the secret. He told that Patrick's grave was at Dún-lethglaise, which we call Downpatrick, a place of ancient fortification in the island plain, and now the municipal town. Possibly the secret came to Columcille from its clerical custodians, and was published by him when danger of scandalous dispute was past.

The precise situation of the grave at Downpatrick is not known, but multitudes of pilgrims down the ages have carried away handfuls of earth from a place in the cathedral graveyard where today, though the cathedral and the consecrated earth are not in Catholic possession, a great uncut granite boulder was laid in our own times, bearing the stark inscription: *Patrie.*

---

1.   Eoin MacNeill, *St. Patrick.*

2. Those Who Remained

Bishop Tassach of Raholp, who gave Patrick the *Viaticum*, was one of the Apostle's metal-workers. He made a case for the *Bachall Iosa*, Patrick's famous crozier. No doubt, he did this after Patrick's death.

Bishop Fiacc of Slethy, the lawyer-convert, who was picked on the advice of Dubthach mac Lugair the poet, when Patrick desired a suitable churchman for episcopal office, and of whom it is told that his poet's memory enabled him to complete his clerical learning in a fortnight, is said to have composed a Gaelic poetical eulogy of Patrick, which is extant under the title *Génair Patraic in Nemthur*, "Patrick was born in Nemthor." The poem which we possess is no older than the eighth century, but we need not doubt that it is based on some piece which came down in tradition. What is likelier than that the Gaels among Patrick's churchmen would lament him in their own tongue, even as Secundinus the Gaul had praised him in Latin?

This Gaelic hymn, which seems to us to be based on a pan-egyric preached, maybe, at the anniversary of the saint's death, recounts the main facts of his life. *Génair Patraic in Nemthur*—Patrick was born in Nemthur, it begins, though this name cannot be explained. It tells how the son of Calpurn was taken prisoner at sixteen, dwelt for six years in bondage, travelled, fasted "in the isles of the Tyrrhene Sea," lived with Germanus, heard the call to Ireland, came, suffered, and taught. Great stress it lays on Patrick's teaching by example as well as word, and his mortifications. "The stormy cold withheld him not from vigils in pools of the river; to win his kingdom in heaven, he preached by day on the hills; on bare flag-stones he reposed, with drenched bedding about him, his bolster a pillar-stone; he allowed his body no warmth." How he prayed, singing a hundred psalms every night, Fiacc tells, and the Roman Breviary today repeats the account of this most active of Apostle's strong interior life. The panegyric tells how Patrick died—our own account is taken from Fiacc—and how a radiance remained over the countryside till the year's end. "The clergy of Ireland travelled by every road to Patrick's wake"—so multitudinous was the attendance. The panegyric ends: "Patrick without proud hauteur (*cen áirde n-uabhair*), great was the goodness of his thoughts (i.e., his interior life); he was in the service of the Son of Mary—that was the good purpose of his birth."

Benignus, in the See of Armagh, survived Patrick four years. Iserninus, the last of the three Gallic coadjutors, outlived Benignus by three years; and, on his death in 468, the chief figures of the mission all had passed away. However, Bishop Mel of Ardagh lived till 488, Cianan of Duleek till 489, and Mac Cairthinn of Clogher until 506.

The ardour and splendour of the Patrician period did not cease with the Apostle and his fellow workers. The history of the Church in ancient Ireland was divided by the ancient native historians into three periods, in which three "Orders" of saints flourished. The first of these, called *sanctissimus*, began in the fifth century with Patrick and lasted until the year 544, when the last of the pagan High-Kings died. The saints of this Order, we are told, "were sprung from the Romans and Franks (Gauls) and Britons and Scots (Irish)." That is to say, they were largely made up of missionaries. They included, however, some of the most illustrious of the native saints, such as St. Enda of Aran, the first true Irish monastic, and, above all, the glorious St. Brigid, who lived until the year 521 or 524. Some have thought that the noble Irish lady whom Patrick specially mentions in his narrative concerning the holy women of

Ireland, was Brigid herself; one legend says that he baptised her. This we may doubt, since the chronology of the saints' lives seems to forbid it; but, undoubtedly she was born before he died, so that her life carries on the light of his sanctity without a break.

We shall see, in a forthcoming study of St. Columcille, that the Irish Church went through a grave ordeal at the end of the age of the First Order, and that the latter half of the sixth century belonged to the labours of the Second Order of Saints, great founders of monastic schools, who built up the Church afresh. Since Patrick's name is not mentioned often in the records of the second period, some writers say that his memory passed under a cloud, from which it did not recover until it was invoked in the seventh and eighth centuries, in the movement to bring Ireland into closer harmony with Rome. This is a reading of history which shows a want of the historic sense. It is only natural that a period of intense activity, like the seventh century, when political development and ecclesiastical construction went on apace, should be filled with the names of the contemporary great men, and that Patrick's person and work should pass for a time, as we would say nowadays, out of the news. The mighty figures of the nineteenth century, in all walks of life, are little mentioned in our own turbulent century; our minds are so much occupied by the rapid changes around us that we are forgetting the Newmans, Lincolns, Parnells, for the time being, although it is certain that writers in the next century will restore the due proportions. We lay no weight, therefore, on the theory of a departure from Patrick and a return to him; but it is true that the exaltation of his cult set in with a fresh fervour in a later time.

3. His Biographers

Apart from Patrick's own writings, the Hymn of Secundinus, and the suppositious original of Fiacc's Hymn, the earliest mention of Patrick in any record is in a letter dated 634, which speaks of *Sanctus Patricius, papa noster.* Before the end of the seventh century, Tírechán of Connacht and Muirchú, of an ecclesiastical family of Armagh, wrote *Lives* of Patrick, which are the base of most later biographies. Tírechán received traditions from the aged Bishop St. Ultan of Ardbraccan, who told him, for example, the fact of Patrick's sojourn as a monk at Lérins of the Saints. He travelled in Meath and Connacht to collect further data. He affirmed the commission of Patrick by Pope Celestine. Muirchú's work is ampler, and rests on older documents, now lost.

At Armagh, Patrick's Confession and Epistle and certain *dicta*, together with Muirchú's Life, were preserved in the great Codex which we still possess and call the Book of Armagh. The Book was written at the beginning of the ninth century by a scribe who copied (so he affirms) Patrick's own manuscript.

Before the end of the ninth century there was written in Irish, with extensive Latin passages, a work which we know as the Tripartite Life. This comprises three dissertations on the saint's life and death, intended for use at the three-day festival which was observed annually in his honour. It is episodic and largely legendary, but its fabulous character has been exaggerated by unsympathetic critics. Much of Chapter X in our present study is derived from the Tripartite Life by the simple process of seeking the framework of likelihood in tales that had been embellished by old-time fancy. When we read of the saint dashing a Druid to death in a miraculous act, we take the incident as a rhetorical exaggeration,

which the hearers of the ninth century understood though it puz-
zles the Dry-as-dusts of recent times. "Ooh, he murdered me!" and
"I'm destroyed walking," are commonplaces of present-day speech
in Ireland which might be treated as evidence of atrocity or of
alleged death-and-revival, by the kind of writer who dismisses the
old *Lives* of Patrick as incredible.

In the seventeenth century, the Irish Franciscans of Louvain
(those holy preservers of our religious and national traditions),
compiled the surviving records of the saints of Ireland, in imitation of the Bollandists. Father John Colgan's *Trias Thaumaturga*,
that mighty work on the Three Patrons, gathered together the chief
documents, Latin and Gaelic, on which we rely for our knowledge
of SS. Brigid and Columcille as well as of Patrick.

The Franciscan movement, however, came when the Irish
nation was stricken down for the Penal centuries, and, although
devotion to the Three Patrons burned in the hearts of the outlawed, suffering nation of unnamed martyrs and confessors, yet
all this was hidden and secret. The learned world forgot about
Patrick until Rev. Dr. John Lanigan published his *Ecclesiastical
History of Ireland* in 1822, and the Protestant Dr. James Todd his
St. Patrick, Apostle of Ireland, in 1863. Todd's large and exhaus-
tive work was the beginning of Patrician scholarship, despite its
author's polemical perversity. In defiance of such indisputable and
explicit evidence as Tírechán's, Todd denied the Roman commission, and portrayed Patrick as a sort of primeval Protestant. In our
present study, we have not discussed the view of Patrick and of
Irish history which is held by those worthy folk who succeed in
persuading themselves that Ireland, in the age of Ambrose, Jerome,
Augustine, Celestine, Leo, Germanus, was converted to a different
form of Christianity from that held by the Church Universal; nor

have we tried to fathom the mind which thinks the whole world wrong. Suffice it that Patrick's life and work and character are comprehensible in every phase if we read his story as a chapter in the history of Catholicism, but the attempt to read into it anything but Catholicism forces the evidence, raises insoluble difficulties, and produces what the scholarly judgment must reject.

After Todd, Archbishop Healy of Tuam published in 1905 a monumental Catholic study of our saint's life and writings, and in the same year the agnostic scholar Bury gave the world his immensely important study of the saint, in which he confirmed the Roman commission and Patrick's visit to Rome. The recent development of Gaelic scholarship led to the works of Rev. John Ryan, S.J., Professor Eoin MacNeill, Dr. Helena Concannon, and Mr. Benedict Fitzpatrick—the works by which our own study has been keyed. Finally, Dr. Oliver St. John Gogarty's *I Follow Saint Patrick*, which appeared while we were working on this book, flung the vivid light of an essayist and traveller's intuition on much that time has obscured, and demonstrated how the slave-boy of Slemish can captivate and dominate the most modern of men, and can send an aviator skimming over Saul in discovery.

4. "So Shall Thy Seed Be"

Across fifteen centuries, then, Patrick speaks to living men, and after so long, his cult is stronger than ever. Our study has failed if it has not revealed the distinctness of his personality. It has been said that the greatest of his miracles was his life. It is a true saying. Saving stories of contests with the Druids at Tara, in which he resorted to fire-walking and similar prodigies—late stories, manifestly imitated from the story of Moses—there is little that we have discarded on the score of doubtful credibility; but as we went through the records a clear, realistic portrait rose before us, of a man who was as human and homely as St. John Bosco; strongly individual, quick to anger and quick to humility; a man who was convinced of a mission and sacrificed all his affections to pursue it, self-condemned to a lonely life, yet compensated by love of God and of his adopted country. Above all, he was a mystic, in a strict Catholic sense. His life demonstrates, more than that of almost any other saint, the workings of Divine Providence in the fortunes of one who was completely dedicated to the divine will; and the many stories of supernatural interior communication bear the stamp of truth.

We saw that Patrick claimed to have been promised that his converts should retain the faith to the end of time. The fidelity of the Irish people, through centuries of persecution, surely gives weight to the promise. Today, Patrick's spiritual descendants out-number those of any save the first Apostles. "Today in the United States and Canada, Australia and South Africa, there are millions of Catholics of Irish blood and Irish priests by the thousand, and nearly one third of the total episcopate of the Catholic Church bear Irish names."[2]

Of churches dedicated to St. Patrick, there are some hundreds in Continental Europe, relics of the great Irish missions of the Middle Ages. At home in Ireland there are one hundred sixty-six, and in Great Britain there are seventy-three. In the United States of America, however, where most of the mighty missionary's spiritual children live, there are four hundred sixty-one churches of

---

2.   Philip Hughes, *A History of the Church*, Volume I.

St. Patrick, including the Cathedrals of New York, El Paso, Lead, Rochester, and Corpus Christi. In Canada, there are sixty-five churches of St. Patrick, including the cathedral at Hamilton, Ontario. In Australia, there are one hundred sixty-four, including the Cathedrals of Melbourne, Ballarat, Perth, and Toowoomba. There are many in New Zealand, South America, the British West Indies, Africa, India, and the Far East. How aptly, therefore, is this scriptural text recited as Offertory in the Mass for St. Patrick's Day: "Look up and number the stars, if thou art able. And He said to him: So shall thy seed be."

EPILOGUE

COLLECT: O God, who dost vouchsafe to send blessed Patrick, Thy Confessor and Bishop, to preach Thy glory to the nations: giant, through his merits and intercession, that what Thou commandest us to do, we may by Thy mercy be able to accomplish. Through our Lord.

SECOND NOCTURN—LESSONS: Patrick, called the Apostle of Ireland, whose father was Calphurnius, and whose mother was Conchessa, a relative, it is said, of S. Martin, Bishop of Tours, was born in greater Britain, and as a boy several times fell into captivity with the barbarians. When in that condition, being put in charge of their grazing flocks, he already gave signs of future holiness; for, filled with faith and the fear of God and the spirit of love, he would diligently rise before dawn, in snow, and host, and rain, to pour forth prayers to God. It was his custom to pray to God a hundred times during the day, and a hundred during the night. After his third deliverance from slavery, he entered the clerical state, and applied himself, for a considerable time, to the study of sacred works. Having made several most fatiguing journeys through

Gaul, Italy, and the Islands of the Tyrrhenian Sea, at last he was called by a divine intimation to the salvation of the Irish; and having power from the blessed Pope Celestine to preach the Gospel, and being consecrated bishop, he proceeded to Ireland.

It is a marvel how much this apostolic man had to endure in this mission; how many evils, how many hardships and labours, how many enemies. But, favoured by the mercy of God, that land, which heretofore had worshipped idols, soon brought forth such fruit from Patrick's preaching that it was afterwards called the Island of the Saints. Very many people were regenerated in the holy font by him; bishops and many clerics were ordained; rules were drawn up for virgins and widows living in continency. By the authority of the Roman Pontiff he appointed Armagh as the chief metropolitan see of the whole island, and enriched it with relics of saints, brought from the City. Moreover, Patrick so shone forth, adorned by God with heavenly visions, with the gift of prophecy, and great signs and wonders, that his fame became more and more celebrated, and spread itself far and wide.

Besides his daily care of the churches, his invincible spirit never slackened in prayer. For it is said that he was wont to recite every day the whole Psalter, together with the Canticles and Hymns, and two hundred prayers; that he every day knelt down three hundred times to adore God; and that at each canonical hour of the day, he signed himself a hundred times with the sign of the cross. He divided the night into three parts; first, he repeated the first hundred Psalms, and genuflected two hundred times; the second was spent in reciting the remaining fifty Psalms, standing in cold water, with his heart, eyes, and hands lifted up to heaven; the third he gave to a little sleep, stretched upon a bare stone. Remarkable for his practice of humility, like the Apostles, he did not abstain from manual labour. At length, worn out by his incessant cares for the Church, glorious in word and work, in extreme old age, he fell asleep in the Lord, after being refreshed with the divine mysteries. He was buried at Down, in Ulster, in the fifth century of the Christian era.

Made in the USA
Monee, IL
26 January 2025

10051983R10115